The Funniest People in Sports: 250 Anecdotes

David Bruce

Published by David Bruce, 2022.

THE FUNNIEST PEOPLE IN SPORTS: 250 ANECDOTES

First edition. October 7, 2022.

ISBN: 979-8215677742

Written by David Bruce.

Table of Contents

Dedication

DEDICATED TO MY SISTER MARTHA

Martha wrote, "When I was working at Longaberger, I worked with a girl who had two children and was in the middle of a divorce. She was so worried about Christmas for her boys. I received a very nice Christmas bonus that year, and I went to my boss and started a donation fund for the girl. My boss told me later that she — my boss — delivered the money to the girl's mother and father and told them not to tell her who brought the money for her. Months later the girl told me that the boys had the best Christmas that year, and she told me someone had brought money to her mom and dad for her, and she went to town and bought the boys Christmas. She never did know who did that for her. She was so thankful. I believe that I was the only one who donated to her, which was just fine."

***

The doing of good deeds is important. As a free person, you can choose to live your life as a good person or as a bad person. To be a good person, do good deeds. To be a bad person, do bad deeds. If you do good deeds, you will become good. If you do bad deeds, you will become bad. To become the person you want to be, act as if you already are that kind of person. Each of us chooses what kind of person we will become. To become a good person, do the things a good person does. To become a bad person, do the things a bad person does. The opportunity to take action to become the kind of person you want to be is yours.

Bai Juyi went to Zen master Daolin of the Tang Dynasty and asked what one must do in order to live in accord with the Tao. Daolin answered, "One must avoid doing evil, and one must do as much good as possible." Bai Juyi was surprised at the simplicity of this answer and said, "Even a child knows that." "True," replied Daolin, "even a child of three knows this but even a man of 80 fails to live up to it."

A seeker after truth once asked a wise person how to seek God. The wise person replied, "The ways to God are as many as there are created beings. But the shortest and easiest is to serve others, not to bother others, and to make others happy."

The Zen master Gisan was taking a bath. The water was too hot, so he asked a student to add some cold water to the bath. The student brought a bucket of cold water, added some cold water to the bath, and then threw the rest of the water on a rocky path. Gisan scolded the student: "Everything can be used. Why did you waste the rest of the water by pouring it on the path? There are some plants nearby which could have used the water. What right do you have to waste even a drop of water?" The student became enlightened and changed his name to Tekisui, which means "Drop of Water."

"While walking along a river, two monks noticed a lettuce leaf floating downstream. "How sad," said one of the monks, who knew that Zen master Gisan lived one mile upstream. "Gizan has started to waste food." Just then, Gisan burst out of the bushes, panting and sweating, jumped into the river, and began to swim downstream after the lettuce leaf. The two monks bowed low in the direction of Zen master Gisan, then they continued their walk.

Public Domain Cover Photograph for *The Funniest People in Sports: 250 Anecdotes*:

Jim Thorpe

https://en.wikipedia.org/wiki/Jim_Thorpe#/media/ File:Jim_Thorpe_Canton_Bulldogs_1915-20.jpg

All anecdotes have been retold in my own words to avoid plagiarism.

Anecdotes are usually short humorous stories. Sometimes they are thought-provoking or informative, not amusing.

At Ohio University is a steep hill by Morton Hall. The last time I rode my bicycle up the hill was in 2016, when the Cleveland Cavaliers were behind 3-1 to the Golden State Warriors. A student saw me reach the top of the hill on my bicycle and said, "If this old man can ride up this hill, the Cavs can make a comeback and win the NBA Championship. The Cavs won three games in a row and won the NBA Championship.

Chapter 1: From Activism to Coaches

Activism

• In 1966, women were not allowed to run in the Boston Marathon. Fortunately, an "uppity" woman did not let that stop her. Roberta Gibb (Bingay) (a rather apt last name) traveled to Boston by bus from California to compete. Of course, she was not allowed to stand at the starting line, so she hid in some bushes near the starting line, and when the male runners raced by, she joined them. At first, she wore a hooded sweatshirt to help disguise her gender, but soon she got too warm and took off the sweatshirt. Ms. Bingay ran the marathon in three hours and twenty-one minutes, finishing 124th in a race in which 415 men competed. Ms. Bingay's running the Boston Marathon had positive results. The following year, another woman ran the marathon unofficially, and in 1972, women were finally allowed to compete officially in the Boston Marathon.[1]

• Tennis star Billie Jean King led a boycott of the United States Lawn Tennis Association by women tennis players. The boycott occurred for a very good reason: the inequality of prize money won by male and by female tennis players. For example, in the 1970 Pacific Southwest Championships, the male champion won $12,500, while the female champion won only $1,500! The boycott worked. Billie Jean King and the other women tennis players competed in a new tennis tournament sponsored by Virginia Slims cigarettes, and they forced the USLTA to recognize the Virginia Slims Invitational.[2]

• In 1971, an unusual raffle was held — the winner got to send 5,000 dead fish to the polluter of his or her choice. The dead fish came from Escambia Bay, and they died in a giant fish kill caused by pollution. Holding the raffle for the huge bottle of dead fish at the Pensacola (Florida) Interstate Fair was the Bream Fisherman Association.[3]

• In 1973, African-American tennis star Arthur Ashe played in a tournament in South Africa, which then practiced a form of segregation known as apartheid. Before he would play in the tournament, Mr. Ashe demanded that the audiences watching it be integrated.[4]

Alcohol

• While Bo Jackson attended Auburn University, he played both baseball and football. During a baseball game at the University of Alabama, a beer truck was parked just beyond the fence around the outfield. Several people, including the driver, were standing by the truck, drinking beer and yelling insults at Mr. Jackson throughout the early innings of the game. Mr. Jackson stopped the insults by hitting a home run that bounced off the side of the truck.[5]

• At a caddie tournament at the Royal and Ancient Golf Club at St. Andrews in Scotland, first prize was a turkey and second prize was a bottle of whiskey. Andrew "Andra'" Kirkaldy and his brother, Hugh Kirkaldy, were ahead of the pack at the last hole. To win the tournament, Hugh needed a five, but instead he deliberately took seven, saying, "Andra' can have the turkey — the bottle of whiskey is more in my line!"[6]

Animals

• Canadian figure skater Toller Cranston once lived in a house in a very bad part of Toronto. On the street outside his house, prostitutes freely worked their trade. One day, Mr. Cranston's pet dog, Minkus, an English setter, turned up missing. Mr. Cranston was frantic, and as he searched the neighborhood, he enlisted the help of every prostitute and every street person he could find. He remembers one Danish prostitute telling a john who tried to buy her wares, "I can't. I'm looking for a dog," as she teetered down an alley on stiletto heels. Eventually, the dog, which had been stolen, was found, and Mr. Cranston had a cocktail party for all the prostitutes and street people who had helped him in the search. At the party, all the guests — men and women — were on their best behavior, saying, "Can I pass this?" and "Can I wash that?" Even though the house was filled with works of art — Mr. Cranston was an artist and an art collector — nothing was stolen.[7]

• In 1971, Bill Pickett became the first African American to be inducted into the National Rodeo Cowboy Hall of Fame, which is located at the Western Heritage Center in Oklahoma City, Oklahoma. Mr. Pickett invented the rodeo event known as bulldogging, in which a cowboy grabs a steer by the horns, twists them, and forces the steer to fall to the ground. Mr. Pickett's style of bulldogging was different from that used today. He used to grab the steer by the horns, bite into its upper lip, then throw himself to the ground. Invariably, the steer would follow. He came up with this idea by watching dogs handle longhorn cattle, which often hid in brush where a cowboy could not lasso them. The dogs would bite into the steer's upper lip and hold the steer until the cowboy arrived. Today, biting into a steer's upper lip is banned as being cruel to the steer.[8]

• Back in the 1970s, a race tracker was envious of jockey Mary Bacon's car, a Toronado, so he asked her, "You got some man supporting you to be able to afford a car like that?" Ms. Bacon worked hard riding horses to be able to afford that car, so she replied, "Yeah. He's got four legs and he's standing in barn 43. Name's John the Hiker. All you got to do is hit him on the *ss and he runs. You hit a two-legger in the *ss and he just stands there."[9]

Audiences

• As a competitor, the most extraordinary moment of figure skating that Toller Cranston ever saw involved a very ill Bob McAvoy and his pairs partner, Mary Petrie. Mr. McAvoy's dream was to go to the World Championships, and he had the opportunity to do just that in Ljubljana, Yugoslavia, in 1970. Unfortunately, he became very ill on the plane trip to Yugoslavia and went straight to a hospital as soon as he arrived. Nevertheless, he forced himself to compete on the ice. The first half of the performance went well, but then Mr. McAvoy's illness caught up with him, making him weak, and he dropped his partner on the ice as he himself fell. The two lay on the ice for a few seconds as their music continued playing, then they got up, bruised and bleeding from their fall. Mr. McAvoy made a gesture to his partner that asked, "Would you like to continue?" Ms. Petrie did, and at this point the audience came alive, cheering them on with such enthusiasm that they skated the performance of a lifetime, followed by an enormous ovation from the crowd. Their scores reflected their fall, but Mr. Cranston says, "It was a moment when skating took a back seat to integrity, sportsmanship, and the belief that nothing is impossible to a willing heart."[10]

• Believe it or not, changing your hairstyle suddenly can put you at a disadvantage in competitive gymnastics. In Moscow, at the 1958 World Championships, Soviet gymnast Polina Astakhova suddenly decided to change to a more fashionable hairstyle, so instead of pulling her hair back into a bun as she usually did, she wore pigtails decorated with blue ribbons. Unfortunately, because of the change in hairstyles, the audience did not recognize her and so they did not give her the burst of applause that can be so helpful in releasing adrenaline and influencing judges. Of course, as soon as she was able, she went back to her usual hairstyle, and the audience recognized her and gave her the usual ovation.[11]

Autographs

• Ohio State University football coach Woody Hayes once visited the troops in Vietnam to boost their morale. During one stop, he spoke to the troops, then asked if there was anyone from Ohio who was not able to be present because of duty. After finding out that an Ohio soldier was on guard duty in an unsafe zone, Mr. Hayes insisted that a helicopter take him to the soldier, where he attempted to autograph a photograph for the soldier but discovered that his only pen was out of ink. He told the soldier, "Come see me when you get home and I'll finish signing the picture." Three years later, the ex-soldier was attending Ohio State University. When he went to Mr. Hayes' office, the coach wasn't there, but the ex-soldier did leave his telephone number. After attending classes, the soldier went home and found Mr. Hayes waiting for him. Mr. Hayes finished signing the photograph, then stayed for a dinner of macaroni and cheese with the ex-soldier and his wife.[12]

• Figure skater Carol Heiss won five gold medals at the World Championships, a silver medal at the 1956 Olympics, and a gold medal at the 1960 Olympics. Oddly, to many people only one of those medals means anything. One day, at the Winterhurst Figure Skating Club in Lakewood, Ohio, a woman came in who didn't know Ms. Heiss. They started talking, and the woman discovered that Ms. Heiss had won the silver medal at the 1956 Olympics. The woman said, "Oh, that's too bad ... what did you go on to do after that?" Ms. Heiss said that she had continued to compete and had won Olympic gold in 1960. Hearing this, the woman was suddenly impressed and wanted Ms. Heiss' autograph. Ms. Heiss gave her the autograph, but she also told her, "I'm very proud of my silver medal in 1956. First time I made the Olympic team, and I'm on the podium."[13]

• As an 11-year-old, gymnast Shannon Miller finished second (behind Wendy Bruce) in the all-around competition in the Alamo Classic. Afterward, the pre-teen Shannon signed autographs for her adoring fans. In fact, when her father, Ron, went up to talk to her, other parents grew angry at him because they thought he was cutting in line.[14]

• In 1992, Dominique Moceanu, then a member of the junior national gymnastics team, had her goal set to compete in the 1996 Olympic Games in Atlanta, Georgia. When asked by fans to sign her autograph, she often wrote, "Dominique Moceanu, Atlanta Olympics, for sure!" She won a team gold medal in Atlanta.[15]

• "Shoeless Joe" Jackson was one of baseball's greatest hitters in the early 1900s, but he was also nearly illiterate and sometimes signed his name with an "X." Frequently, fans would mail requests for autographed baseballs to his house, but it was his wife, Katie, who signed his name to the baseballs.[16]

• Gordon Gee, the former president of the Ohio State University, looks like Lou Holtz, the coach of the Notre Dame football team. One day, someone asked Mr. Gee for his autograph, which he willingly gave. The fan looked at the autograph, then asked, "Who are you? I thought you were Lou Holtz."[17]

Birth

• When Russian ice skater Ekaterina Gordeeva was giving birth in New Jersey to her daughter (Daria), she was in terrific pain. Her doctor offered to give her a shot to make the pain go away, but she had to read and sign a form — written in English, of course — first. Ekaterina's husband, Sergei Mikhailovich Grinkov, didn't speak English, and because she was in such great pain, she wasn't able to read the form (at that point, she wasn't able to think in English anymore). Still, because she wanted the pain to go away, she signed the form, even though she was afraid that the form would maybe also make her car and her Rolex go away.[18]

• A friend of Quaker humorist Tom Mullen was a sports nut with an expectant wife. He said that he didn't care whether the baby was a boy or a girl, but many people thought he would prefer a boy because he loved sports so much. When his child — a daughter — was born, the sports nut called up all his friends and said, "You ought to see her hands. They're great! She'll be the best girl basketball player in Indiana!"[19]

Children and Teenagers

• Olympic gold medalist figure skater Tara Lipinski started out as a roller skater. She began to ice skate only on a fluke. This is what happened. The mother of a friend of Tara's wanted Tara to start figure skating because the future of a roller skater — even a champion roller skater — was limited. (Roller skating is not an Olympic event.)

However, Tara's mother resisted the idea because there weren't any good ice rinks near where they lived and Tara's taking ice skating lessons would be very inconvenient. But she decided to let Tara go ice skating just once to prove to Tara's friend's mother that Tara would be terrible at it. Sure enough, Tara was terrible at first and fell down a lot. Relieved, her parents went out for hot chocolate. But when they returned 45 minutes later, Tara had figured out how to skate and was doing axels and waltz jumps and was skating backwards. The other skaters were amazed at how much she had progressed in just 45 minutes. Instead of being terrible at ice skating, Tara was hooked on it and began taking lessons.[20]

• When Summer Sanders was two years old, her parents installed a swimming pool. Of course, this led to a problem — how could they keep Summer safe? They tried giving her swimming lessons, but it seemed that Summer preferred to cry rather than listen to her teacher, so her parents gave up on the swimming lessons, bought her flotation devices for her arms, and prepared to keep an eye on her whenever she was near the pool. However, Summer surprised them one day by taking off the flotation devices, jumping into the pool, and swimming. She had been paying attention to her teacher after all. The lessons and swimming pool paid off in a big way — Summer became a gold medalist in the butterfly at the 1992 Olympic Games in Barcelona, Spain.[21]

• Eric Gregg, the third black umpire in the major leagues, got an early lesson in umpiring while working a Little League game early in his career. Billy, a seven-year-old kid playing for a team being battered 21-1, came up to bat and told him, "Mister, you see that guy coaching third base? That's my dad. I've struck out three times today, and if I strike out again, he's really gonna let me have it." With a full count on the kid, a pitch was close enough to be called a strike, but Mr. Gregg called it a ball and the kid walked. Later, he started to tell the other umpires about the kid, and they knew immediately who the kid was: "Billy! That kid get you, too? He pulls that sh*t every week! You didn't give him a free walk, did you?"[22]

• Muhammad Ali, whose name at birth was Cassius Clay, began to box as a result of someone stealing his bicycle. He had gone into an auditorium to attend a bazaar, and when he got out his bike was gone. He complained to police officer Joe Martin and said, "If I find the kid who stole my bike, I'll whip him!" Mr. Martin, an amateur boxing coach, suggested, "If you plan to whip somebody, maybe you'd better come down [to the gym] and learn how." The young Cassius took Mr. Martin's advice. He never did find out who had stolen his bike, but he challenged a neighborhood bully to a fight and busted his nose. After the fight, he and his friends stopped fearing the bully.[23]

• When Lynette Woodard was five years old, one of her cousins, Geese Ausbie, told her about his experiences playing for the Harlem Globetrotters, and so young Lynette wanted to play for the Harlem Globetrotters. She practiced her cousin's basketball tricks around the house as she grew up, with the result that she broke many things around the house as she grew up. However, the practice paid off. She became a scoring sensation at Kansas University, finishing her collegiate career with 3,649 points. In addition, in 1985, she became the first female Globetrotter, debuting on October 17 in a game played in Brisbane, Australia.[24]

• When American gymnast Dominique Moceanu was only six months old, her parents (who had been gymnasts in Romania before coming to the United States to live) tested her strength by having her grab onto a clothesline and hang on by herself. Of course, her mother was ready to catch her if she let go of the clothesline — but she never did. After witnessing this demonstration of her strength, her parents decided that Dominique could probably be a top gymnast. She proved them right by winning a gold medal at the 1996 Olympics in Atlanta.[25]

• When the Romanian junior women's gymnastics team flew to New York to participate in the 2000 Pontiac Women's Gymnastics Team Championships, the flight attendants were happy to have such celebrities on board and took photographs of the team. Later, the flight attendants brought coloring books to the Romanian gymnasts, offending them deeply. The gymnasts, who were tiny 14- and 15-year-olds, said, "Hey, we're small, but we're not that young."[26]

• When Olympic gymnast Shannon Miller was a little girl, she started taking gymnastics. One day, the girls at her school took part in a parade. Little Shannon noticed some of the other girls doing back walkovers, so she decided to do them, too. Unfortunately, this was a skill she hadn't quite mastered yet, so whenever she wanted to attempt a back walkover, her mother ran out of the audience and spotted her to make sure she wouldn't land on her head.[27]

• In 1971, when they were kids, gymnasts Bart Conner and Jim Hartung competed against each other. Young Bart was amazed by the size of young Jim's ears, so he got behind him and took a photograph of the back of his head so he could show Jim's ears to his friends. Later, the rest of Jim's body caught up with his ears, the two continued to compete against each other in college, and the two became Olympic gold medal-winning teammates in Los Angeles.[28]

• Even at age six, Olympic gold medalist Shannon Miller was a master at saving time. She used to wear her leotard underneath her clothing at school to save time dressing for gymnastics practice after school. This trick gave her a few more minutes of precious TV-watching time. (Her parents didn't know she was doing this until they received her school photographs and saw the sleeves of her leotards poking out underneath the sleeves of her dress.)[29]

• Even before Jennifer Capriati was a teenager, she showed great toughness and determination as a tennis player. During practice, her tennis-training partner hit a hard drive that smacked into her forehead. Young Jennifer lowered her head, raised her hand, wiped her eye, then got right back into the ready position — even though tears were flowing from her eyes. In 1992, Ms. Capriati won an Olympic gold medal in women's tennis.[30]

• While growing up in West Virginia, Mary Lou Retton learned gymnastics easily. When Mary Lou was six, she tried to teach her sister a trick she had learned at cheerleading camp: a cartwheel without hands, aka a side aerial. Her sister tried it — and broke her arm. At the time, her mother was making snickerdoodles, and Mary Lou's sister refused to eat snickerdoodles thereafter because she associated them with her broken arm.[31]

• When Maria Butyrskaya was 15 years old, her coach at the Central Army Club in Moscow told her that she had no talent and that she should get out of figure skating. Fortunately, Ms. Butyrskaya didn't listen to the coach. She continued to train in figure skating, and in 1999, she became the World Champion — in fact, she was the first Russian woman ever to become World Champion in women's figure skating.[32]

• Even as a toddler, elite gymnast Vanessa Atler loved tumbling classes. Her mother remembers that young Vanessa was so eager to go to class that she used to put on her leotard hours before practice. (By the way, young Vanessa almost became an ice skater, but her mother enrolled her in gymnastics classes because the Atler family couldn't afford to buy ice skates for her.)[33]

• Greg Maddux played for the Chicago Cubs and the Atlanta Braves, as well as for other teams. As a 12-year-old Little Leaguer, he was so gifted a pitcher that his coach would not allow him to pitch in a championship game, saying that allowing him to pitch would not be fair to the other team! (Greg played, but did not pitch, and his team won the championship.)[34]

• In 1990, when tennis player Jennifer Capriati was 14 years old, she played against Martina Navratilova in the finals of the *Family Circle Magazine Cup* in Hilton Head Island, South Carolina. Ms. Navratilova won both the tournament and the Mazda Miata sports car that went to the champion, then said, "It's just as well I won it — since Jennifer can't drive."[35]

• When Canadian gymnast Elfi Schlegel was seven years old, she won her first competition. As a reward, she was given a trophy, while the second- and third-place competitors were given medals hanging from ribbons. Ms. Schlegel was so young that she was disappointed that she didn't win a medal necklace like her friends had.[36]

• Amy Chow, who won gold (team) and silver (uneven bars) at the 1996 Olympics in Atlanta, got into gymnastics by accident. When Amy was three years old, her mother wanted her to take dance lessons, but the dance studio thought she was too young for lessons, so her mother enrolled her in a gymnastics class instead.[37]

• When Evonne Goolagong was a child in Australia, she entered what she thought was a tennis tournament for children in Narrandera. However, when she arrived at the tournament, she discovered that it was for adults. No problem. She played in the tournament anyway — and won![38]

• Shannon Martin was six years old when she won an age-12-and-under roping contest, for which she was written up in the *Roping Sports News*. Because she hadn't learned to read yet, she kept saying to her father, "Come on, Dad. Read it again."[39]

Christmas

• As a youngster in an impoverished family, golfer Sam Snead suffered through some bleak Christmases. Sometimes, he found his Christmas presents under a plate — two or three nickels. Other times his Christmas present was a pair of socks. What was his best-ever Christmas present? A sled his father had made for him.[40]

Clothing

• Track and field star Florence Griffith Joyner was known for her outrageous racing clothes and painted fingernails as well as for her wins and world records. For example, at the 1988 Olympic Trials at the Indiana University Track Stadium, she wore a one-legged, green bodysuit and a one-legged, turquoise-and-purple bodysuit. In addition, for one race, she painted her long fingernails mostly orange — at their ends she painted black and white stripes. At the 1988 Olympic Games in Seoul, Korea, she wore a fluorescent blue-and-white outfit as well as an all-lace bodysuit that resembled a negligee. At the 1984 Olympic Games in Los Angeles, she painted nine fingernails red, white, and blue, and one fingernail gold — the color of the medal she hoped to win. Actually, in 1984 she won the silver medal in the 200-meter race, but in 1988 she won the gold.[41]

• At Michelle Kwan's first United States Nationals ice skating championship tournament, her coach, Frank Carroll, was shocked at the condition of her unshined skating boots. Immediately, he started shouting for boot polish to shine her boots because he was afraid that the skating judges would regard the unshined boots as an insult to them. While the other coaches were laughing, Mr. Carroll shined Michelle's boots and blew on them to make them dry. When she skated in the competition, her boots were still wet. (Ms. Kwan hadn't meant any disrespect. At that time, she believed in the superstition that you should not shine your boots while you are performing well.)[42]

• Barbara Underhill and Paul Martini are a sexually charged pairs skating couple. Ms. Underhill is a beautiful woman, and Mr. Martini is a hunk. During one session to work out the pair's choreography for "When a Man Loves a Woman," an embarrassed Mr. Martini had to stand still while Ms. Underhill and choreographer Sandra Bezic had fun figuring out — and demonstrating — the best way for Ms. Underhill to grab his butt during the performance. In the finished program, Mr. Martini wore blue jeans, and Ms. Underhill stood in front of him, reached around him, and put her hands in his rear pockets.[43]

• Underneath their colored stockings, professional baseball players wear white sanitary hose. Why? In and before 1905, players wore only the socks bearing the colors of their team. However, in 1905, a player sliding into second base cut Napoleon Lajoie's foot. The dye from his colored socks seeped into the wound and he came down with a bad case of blood poisoning. He survived and continued to play baseball, but as a precautionary measure players began to wear white sanitary hose.[44]

• While playing at the Jerry Ford Invitational Golf Tournament in Vail, Colorado, baseball great Yogi Berra split his pants. The crowd was amused to see that Mr. Berra was wearing Yogi Bear undershorts.[45]

Coaches

• In figure skating, people fiercely compete to get the best coach. The mother of a young figure skater once telephoned Frank Carroll, who has coached Michelle Kwan, at 2:30 a.m., although he was asleep and had to get up at 4:30 a.m. The skating mother explained, "I thought this was the only time that I could get through to you." Mr. Carroll responded by living without a telephone for the next three years.[46]

• Michelle Kwan is a United States and World Champion figure skater. From her coach, Frank Carroll, she has learned to keep going after a fall — even during practice. According to Mr. Carroll, a fall can be the most important part of a practice, because it may be the only time you ever practice continuing to a strong finish in your program after recovering from that particular fall.[47]

• A Notre Dame basketball team played badly, trailing 15 points at halftime. Coach George Keogan angrily and methodically ripped each player apart at halftime, going from one to the other in order. Finally, he looked at Marty Peters and asked, "What have you got to say for yourself?" Mr. Peters replied, "Only this, coach — I haven't gotten into the game yet."[48]

• Bob Zuppke coached the football Illini for years. In a discussion of football rules, someone described a play and asked whether the officials had made the right call. Before answering, however, Mr.

Zuppke asked, "Which team made the foul — Illinois or the other one?"[49]

Chapter 2: From Comedians to Fathers

Comedians

• A baseball player named Thurman Tucker, a White Sox outfielder, looked a lot like the famous comedian Joe E. Brown. One day, Mr. Brown watched a game in which Mr. Tucker went to bat 9 times, but made only one hit. After the game, Mr. Brown went to the White Sox clubhouse, where he told Mr. Tucker, "Look, if you're going to look like me, hit like me." Mr. Tucker replied, "I'm afraid that's just what I've been doing."[50]

• Groucho Marx once captained a charity baseball game between the Comedians and the Actors. He ordered Jack Benny to step up to the plate and hit a home run, but Mr. Benny promptly struck out. This caused Groucho to resign, complaining, "I can't manage a team that won't follow instructions."[51]

• When Jackie Gleason was a struggling nightclub comedian, famous ice skater Sonja Henie walked in during one of his performances. Mr. Gleason handed her an ice cube and said, "Do something."[52]

Competitiveness

• The longest winning streak ever in college sports — 131 straight games in the 1950s — is held by the Flying Queens of Wayland Baptist College in Plainview, Texas. This team, coached by Harley Redin, did a Harlem Globetrotter-type warmup before games, and they were so famous that the school bought them a private plane so they could perform exhibitions across the country. In 1958, the Flying Queens played Nashville Business College in the AAU championship game, and Nashville Business College won, despite a valiant come-from-behind effort by the Flying Queens. With 15 seconds left on the clock, the game definitely lost, and many players on the team crying because their 131-game winning streak was over, Coach Redin called time out. He told his players — tears streaming from their eyes

— in the huddle, "I called time out so I could tell you this. I want you to go back out there and lose. And I want you to lose with the same kind of class that you've won with for the past five years." This is the moment the players on the team most remember — and remember as thrilling.[53]

• In 1996, the United States "Magnificent Seven" women's gymnastics team won the gold medal at the Olympics Games held in Atlanta. The team had a big lead heading into their final event, the vault, but Dominique Moceanu sat down on both of her vaults and Kerry Strug injured herself on her first vault, which scored poorly. Although the U.S. had already clinched the gold medal, no one knew that for sure, so Ms. Strug had to decide whether to attempt another vault despite being injured. She went for it, completed a high-scoring vault, then collapsed in pain. Later, when the decision to attempt the vault was criticized, she said, "I'm 18 years old — it was my decision." Her coach, Bela Karolyi, was impressed by her courage, saying, "I had not seen this previously in her."[54]

• Joe Kirkwood and Walter Hagen performed a lot of golf exhibitions together. Good friends, they roomed together, and they played games together. One game they played while rooming in a hotel by Central Park was to each hit a golf ball out of the hotel window into the park, go out to the balls, and play them back into the hotel, through the lobby, up the stairs, into their room, into the bathroom, and for a big finish, into the toilet. According to Mr. Kirkwood, "Walter and I were pretty evenly matched until we got into the bathroom. Walter could never get the ball into the can. It drove him crazy."[55]

• Before the 1997 United States National Figure Skating Championships, coach Richard Callaghan suggested to skater Tara Lipinski that she try to perform a difficult triple loop-triple loop jump. This combination had been performed in competition by only one man — it had never been performed in competition by a woman. Its difficulty lies in the fact that the skater must take off and land using the same foot in succession and the first triple loop must be performed perfectly in order to set up the second. Tara agreed to try the difficult combination, and on her first attempt, she landed it.[56]

• As a young gymnast, Svetlana Boginskaya was intensely competitive, even engaging in mind games such as staring at competing gymnasts and never smiling in an attempt to psych out her opponents. As a little girl, she sometimes kicked and bit other gymnasts who she thought were more capable than her. In fact, she was such a terror that the mothers of the other gymnasts used to bring her candy in an attempt to bribe her to be nice to their children. Young Svetlana used to eat the candy but continue to be mean to their children. (Today, she is a well-mannered young woman.)[57]

• In a memorable moment, after Brandi Chastain scored on a penalty kick with her off-foot (she is right-handed, but kicked the penalty goal with her left foot) to give the United States victory in the 1999 World Cup final, she stripped off her shirt, revealing her sports bra. However, because she had missed a penalty shot in an exhibition game a few months previously, she almost was not given the opportunity to make the shot. Fortunately, her World Cup coach, Tony DiCicco, asked her, "Do you think you can make it?" Ms. Chastain answered, "Yeah, I do." The rest is history.[58]

• The best gymnasts know not to quit, no matter what. Larissa Latynina competed during a storm at the 1968 European Championships. The storm knocked out all the electricity, causing the lights to go out, but Ms. Latynina continued her floor exercise even though the judges and audience could see her only when lightning flashed. (Back then, floor routines were not dangerous like they are today, so it was safe for her to continue performing.)[59]

• After Janet Lynn fell twice in the compulsory skating at the 1973 World Championships, failing to win the gold and winning the silver instead, she went to the women's dressing room and cried and cried. She was such a popular figure skater that the other skaters in the dressing room felt her sadness and they also cried — including Karen Magnussen, who won the gold medal.[60]

• Dominique Dawes, a gold medalist as an American team member in the 1996 Olympics Games in Atlanta, competed in her first gymnastics meet at age 10 and won every event! Actually, that's not as impressive as it seems, since only one other person — her best friend — was competing against her. Ms. Dawes remembers the competition well: "It was really funny. We were falling all over the place."[61]

• Joe Venuti played jazz violin much better than he played golf. After hitting the ball into the lake at the Lakeside Golf Club in Hollywood, Mr. Venuti became so frustrated that he threw his club into the water, then he threw his other clubs and golf bag into the water, then he picked up his caddy and threw him into the water, and finally he threw himself into the water.[62]

• Competitive figure skaters must be dedicated — and so must the professional photographers who cover them. At the 1995 World Championships, photographer Gérard Châtaigneau went to the ice dance practice at 5 a.m. All the ice dancers were in costume and all the women ice dancers were already perfectly made up.[63]

• The football players who made up Notre Dame's Four Horsemen contributed greatly to the team's success, but so did the seven players who made up the team's Seven Mules. To decide who contributed more to the team's success, the starting team held a vote. The Seven Mules beat the Four Horsemen — seven votes to four.[64]

• In the late 1920s, the Harlem Globetrotters played a local team that hadn't lost in three years. Before the game, three men with guns told the Globetrotters that the local team had better not lose this game, either. As usual, the Globetrotters won easily — but they made sure after the game to get out of town quickly.[65]

• Athlete Babe Didrikson was definitely cocky. Often, she would show up at a golf tournament and say, "OK, Babe's here! Now who's gonna finish second?" She was able to back up her cockiness. Once, she won a record 17 golf tournaments in a row.[66]

Conversation

• Yogi Berra talked almost constantly when he played catcher for the New York Yankees. In a game against the Boston Red Sox, Yogi kept on talking as Sam Mele was up to bat. Mr. Mele finally turned to umpire Bill Kinnamon and asked, "Bill, can't you get this son of a bitch to shut up?" Mr. Kinnamon replied, "Well, Sam, if he's talking to you, he's not talking to me."[67]

• New York Yankee Yogi Berra was a talker. When he came up to bat, he would frequently ask major league umpire Tom Gorman how his family was, but occasionally Mr. Gorman didn't feel like talking. One game, Mr. Berra asked how his family was, and Mr. Gorman replied, "They died last night. Get in there and hit."[68]

Dedication

• When NBA star Charles Barkley was 15 years old, the coach of his high school basketball team told him that he couldn't jump high enough to play because he was too short and too fat. Young Charles wanted to play basketball, so he decided to teach himself how to jump. In the hot summer sun of Alabama, he ran at a 4-foot-high fence and attempted to jump over it. Sometimes he succeeded, but sometimes he failed, bruising his elbows and knees. His mother even said that her son looked that summer as if he had survived a car accident. Eventually, Charles could stand by the fence and jump it without first getting a running start. His jumping ability came in handy when he played basketball for Leeds High School, Auburn University, the Philadelphia 76ers, and the Houston Rockets.[69]

• Despite being born with only one arm, gymnast Carol Johnston competed for Cal State — Fullerton in Fullerton, California, in the late 1970s. Shortly after learning how to do a double backflip, she injured her wrist and was forced to rest it and not practice gymnastics for two weeks. However, during that time, she mentally visualized herself doing the double backflip and her other gymnastics skills. On her first day of practice after the injury, people expected her to practice only her easier skills, but she did the double backflip twice — perfectly. She said, "I think it shows the power of the mind."[70]

• Murriel Page, a 6-foot-2 forward for the Washington Mystics, a women's professional basketball team, is known for her physical style of play. She acquired it by playing against male cousins and uncles who didn't give her a break because of her gender. They declined to let her shoot baskets over them; instead, they knocked her down.[71]

• Gymnasts frequently show enormous dedication to their sport. In 1994, an earthquake shook California, but elite gymnast Vanessa Atler continued to practice even though her family was forced for a while to sleep in a tent in their backyard. According to Ms. Atler, "Rain or earthquakes, we still have practice."[72]

• As a young boxer, Cassius Clay (who later changed his name to Muhammad Ali) trained intensely. He used to get up at 4 a.m., run, go back to bed, then wake up and go to school. Sometimes, he wouldn't take the school bus, but instead raced it for the 20 blocks to school.[73]

Education

• While practicing the martial art wing-chun, Joe Hyams was accidentally hit by a workout partner. This made him angry. His teacher, Jim Lau, noticed and spoke to him about his anger, saying that unleashing anger against another person inspires anger in return from the other person. The following weekend, Mr. Hyams went to New York, arriving early in the morning and hoping to get some rest before a business meeting. Unfortunately, his hotel room was not ready and would not be ready for another four hours, so he demanded to see the manager, then angrily confronted her. Later, after having calmed down, he apologized, and the manager said, "You really took me by surprise. I intended to do what I could for you, but when you came on so strong I forgot my good intentions and decided not to go out of my way to help you."[74]

• While attending Stanford University, Debi Thomas wasn't sure whether she wanted to enter the 1986 United States National Ice Skating Championships because she had so much schoolwork to do. In fact, when she received the entry form, she tore it up, but then she decided to keep the pieces. Later, she taped the pieces together, filled the form out, then sent it in. It's a good thing she did. She won the gold medal at the Nationals, then she added another gold medal at the World Championships. In 1988, as the first African American on a United States Olympics ice skating team, she earned a bronze medal in Calgary, Alberta, Canada.[75]

• The father of Olympic gold medal-winning gymnast Shannon Miller is a university physics professor. As such, he knows to take a look at the big picture. Whenever Shannon was upset because she didn't get a high enough score on a chemistry test, he would ask her a few questions to test her knowledge. If she knew the answers — she usually did — he would tell her, "So you forgot a few things for one hour, but you told me everything you were supposed to know. What's important is that you learned the material."[76]

• WNBA star Lisa Leslie also excelled at track in high school, although she took a roundabout way of getting on the track team. At Morningside High School in Inglewood, California, she performed the part of track star Wilma Rudolph in a school play. During her performance, she had to run around the auditorium, and she ran so quickly that the track coach invited her to run for the team.[77]

• When Paul Brown, coach of the Cleveland Browns, spoke about the team's philosophy, he expected the players to take notes. Once a player kept talking while Mr. Brown told the players how he expected them to act — that player was traded.[78]

• Many colleges recruited Wilt Chamberlain to play basketball for them, including some schools that asked if he wished to be the first African-American player on their team. Mr. Chamberlain always responded, "I'd rather be the second."[79]

• A football player at Penn State was drafted by the NFL. He asked coach Joe Paterno whether he should play pro football or go to medical school. "Are you nuts?" Mr. Paterno said. "It's only football. Go to medical school, you jerk."[80]

Fans

• A 10-year-old girl, nicknamed Stuffy, lived in Boonton, New Jersey, where she was a fan of the New York Giants football team. She was especially a fan of Y.A. Tittle and was a member of his fan club. At a party she gave for some of the other young members of the fan club, she became so excited that she called Giants Stadium and asked to speak to Mr. Tittle. Sure enough, she was connected with a man who said that he was Y.A. Tittle and talked to her for a while. But later, she wondered whether the man was really Mr. Tittle. A few days later, Stuffy's father took her and her younger sister to a department store where Mr. Tittle was appearing. The younger sister asked Mr. Tittle, "Did you really talk on the phone to Stuffy, my sister?" Mr. Tittle winked and asked, "You mean Stuffy of the Boonton Fan Club?"[81]

• Young figure skaters are naturally awed when they find themselves in the presence of the current world champions. Ice dancers Jayne Torvill and Christopher Dean were certainly awed when they first competed against the world champions, and after Torvill and Dean became world champions, a young Paul Duchesnay, who skated with Isabelle, his sister, was awed to find himself rooming with Mr. Dean in Oberstdorf, Germany. The morning after discovering he was rooming with the current world champion, Mr. Duchesnay heard Mr. Dean arise, but he stayed in bed. Later, he admitted to Mr. Dean, "I just didn't dare move until you'd gone!"[82]

• Auburn University football player Bo Jackson once rear-ended a car, an accident that made the driver of the other car very irate. She told Mr. Jackson that the accident was his fault and that he was a terrible driver. However, as soon as she heard his name, she asked, "Are you the Bo Jackson who plays for Auburn?" He admitted that he was, and she immediately asked, "Are you all right?" As an Auburn football fan, she wanted to make sure that Mr. Jackson could play against the University of Texas. In fact, before the game, she sent Mr. Jackson a note: "Smash Texas like you smashed my car."[83]

• Some of the most popular men's gymnasts have little teenage fans asking for their autographs. After a gymnastics meet, some young girls were waiting around, hoping that Kurt Thomas would sign their autograph books for them. One asked a young woman, "Do you think Kurt will sign my book?" She replied, "Well, I don't know. He's awfully tired and would probably like to get going." The fan then asked, "How do you know so much? Who do you think you are, his mother or something?" The young woman, named Beth, replied, "No, I'm his wife."[84]

• Visiting instructor Rabbi Henry E. Kagan played baseball at a Methodist school in West Virginia in a game pitting the faculty versus the students. With his faculty team one run behind, he was on third. The batter hit a single, and Rabbi Kagan ran for home plate. As he ran, he heard an excited fan shouting, "Come on, Rabbi! Bring home the bacon!" Everyone enjoyed a laugh, and Rabbi Kagan said, "The incident did more than teaching or preaching to instill the idea of brotherhood."[85]

• Some people don't think that Olympic gold medal-winning gymnast Shannon Miller is really Shannon Miller when they unexpectedly see her at the airport or some place other than a gymnasium. One guy asked her, "If you're really Shannon Miller, what was your score on the balance beam at the Olympics finals?" Since she doesn't pay any attention to her scores (and seldom watches programs featuring her performing gymnastics), she was forced to say, "I don't have a clue."[86]

• Michael Jordan was an amazingly popular basketball player for the Chicago Bulls. At home games, attendance rose by 87 percent the first year he played for the Bulls. He was also popular in other cities.

Sometimes, fans of other teams would boo their own players when they fouled Mr. Jordan as he drove to the basket — a foul meant that the fans missed seeing Mr. Jordan dunk the basketball.[87]

• At the 1972 Olympic Games in Sapporo, Japan, Janet Lynn fell on her flying sit-spin — a spin she had practiced and performed thousands of times without mishap. But she got up smiling and won both the bronze medal and the hearts of thousands of Japanese fans watching her. After the Olympics, Janet received many letters written in Japanese, which a Japanese friend translated for her.[88]

• At the 1978 World Championships, gymnast Kurt Thomas won a gold medal in floor exercise — thus winning the United States its first gold medal ever at this level and becoming an instant celebrity. Immediately, he began receiving lots of fan letters from 12- and 13-year-old girls who had developed crushes on him. Each of these letters was answered — by Kurt's wife, Beth.[89]

• After a baseball game at which he had officiated, minor league umpire Harry "Steamboat" Johnson was accosted by a woman who hit him several times with her umbrella. He warded off the blows as best he could, then told the woman, "Lady, I don't know who you are, but if you can get someone to introduce us, you can go on hitting me." She laughed and quit hitting him.[90]

• For many years, Soviet athlete Albert Azaryan was the Lord of the Rings in men's gymnastics. At a national championship tournament, a woman arrived late at the gym and asked, "When is Azaryan performing on the rings?" When she learned that he had already performed his routine, she started crying and explained, "But I only came here because of him."[91]

• Gymnast Vera Cáslavská of Czechoslovakia won seven gold medals at the 1964 and 1968 Olympics Games. During an interview, a reporter asked her about her hobbies. She said that she collected postcards, and within three days after the interview appeared, fans had sent her 3,500 more postcards to add to her collection.[92]

• After winning gold at the 1996 Atlanta Olympics, women's gymnastics teammate Amy Chow became a major celebrity. While attending her first year at Stanford University, she was forced to take her name down from her room in the dormitory because so many students were stopping by to congratulate her on her gold medal.[93]

• At the 1972 Olympic Games in Munich, Soviet gymnast Olga Korbut won several medals and became beloved by the world. As an instant celebrity, she found it difficult to shop for souvenirs for her family in Munich stores. Once, she even tried shopping in a wig and a borrowed maxi dress — but she was still recognized.[94]

• Tallulah Bankhead was born in Alabama. A baseball fan as well as an actress, she worked frequently on Broadway and supported the New York Giants, once telling New York Yankee Lou Gehrig, "I wish I could be a fan of your side. But I just couldn't root for a team named Yankees."[95]

• Charles W. Eliot of Harvard was on his way to attend the Yale-Harvard football game in the company of Edward Everett Hale, when an acquaintance asked where he was going. Dr. Eliot replied, "To yell with Hale."[96]

Fathers

• Lisa Fernandez won an Olympic gold medal as a softball player. Her father supported her from the very beginning, although in Hispanic culture, women's and girls' sports are not emphasized. He took a lot of kidding from his friends because of his athletic daughter, but when her first poster and her first signed Louisville Slugger bat came on the market, he showed them to his friends and said, "This is what my daughter does!" And when she won her Olympic gold medal, he wore it around his neck for several days just so other people would know what his daughter had accomplished.[97]

• Sonja Henie dominated early women's figure skating, winning 10 consecutive world championships and three Olympic gold medals. Her father was a big supporter — he once grabbed a broom and chased an unappreciative skating judge down a street.[98]

Chapter 3: From Fights to Language

Fights

• Patty Barton was a jockey at Waterford Park in West Virginia in the 1970s. She quickly learned that she would have to be tough to make her way as a jockey in a man's world. In fact, she is tough and muscular — she says, "I'm the only mother I know whose kids bring the neighbors in to look at her muscles." In a race, another jockey by the name of Clifford Thompson deliberately knocked into her horse and hit her across her rear end with his whip. After the race, she waited for him. He snuck into the male jockeys' room, and she followed him there, then she started a fight. Blood flowed for a while, and after the fight had been broken up, a steward asked what had caused the fight. Ms. Barton pulled down her pants and underpants and showed the steward the welt caused by her opponent's riding whip. Both jockeys were fined, but Mr. Thompson was fined twice as much as Ms. Barton. (In addition, Ms. Barton was requested in future to ask the track nurse to examine her instead of pulling down her underpants in front of a male steward.) In another fight with a male jockey, she grabbed his genitals. Later, she said, "You go tell that little so-and-so that there was hardly anything to get hold of."[99]

• Cathy Gale is a feminist character in the 1960s British tongue-in-cheek TV series *The Avengers*. Instead of screaming for help when attacked by a thug, Mrs. Gale responded with martial arts, including kicks to the groin. This didn't happen at first. Honor Blackman, who performed the role of Mrs. Gale, disliked some of the early scripts because her character was "so wet." She finally told the writers, "Look, write my part as if I were a man, and I'll turn it into a woman's part."[100]

• Heavyweight boxer Jerry Quarry won a televised match in Madison Square Garden in March of 1969. Unfortunately for the audience watching at home, commercials for a Ford dealership were shown between the rounds of the match, with the commercial cutting off the end of one round and the beginning of the next round. After the fight was over, irritated viewers at home were delighted when, after winning the fight, Mr. Quarry was awarded a new General Motors Pontiac.[101]

• Practitioners of the martial arts are very willing to walk away from fights they know they can easily win. (If they respect their opponent, they will fight.) Martial arts master Tajima once entered a town where news of his arrival quickly spread. A hothead eager to make a name for himself challenged Tajima to a duel to the death, but Tajima replied, "You are too young — and unworthy — to die," then left the town.[102]

• Jackie Robinson, the African-American player who integrated baseball's major leagues, was a fighter no matter what sport he played. While playing basketball for Pasadena Junior College, he faced an opponent who kept sticking his hand in Mr. Robinson's face, including in his mouth. Mr. Robinson grew tired of the abuse, so he bit the opposing player's finger — and bit it hard. This almost caused a riot.[103]

• When Mike Tyson fought Michael Spinks in Atlantic City, New Jersey, Mr. Tyson won quickly. In fact, writer Bill Barich sat near the seat of a man who had purchased a $1,500 ticket but failed to return from the restroom in time to witness any of the 91-second fight.[104]

Firsts

• The Boston Celtics basketball team scored a couple of notable firsts in opening doors to talented African Americans. In 1950, Walter Brown drafted Chuck Cooper, an African-American forward who played for Duquesne University. Another owner of an NBA team tried to convince Mr. Brown not to become the first team owner to draft an African-American player, but Mr. Brown replied, "I don't give a damn if he's striped or polka-dot or plaid — Boston takes Charles Cooper of Duquesne." In addition, when Red Auerbach quit coaching the Celtics, he handpicked center Bill Russell to be his replacement. Mr. Russell thus became the first African-American head coach or manager in a major team sport in the United States. In appreciation for Mr. Russell's talents, the Celtics paid him $100,001 — $1 more than Philadelphia star Wilt Chamberlain received.[105]

• Great Britain's Madge Syers struck a blow for women's liberation when she applied to skate in the world figure skating championship of 1902. Because the rules did not state that a woman couldn't enter the competition, in which only men customarily competed, the judges allowed her to skate. She finished second to Sweden's Ulrich Salchow, and defeated the male skaters from Germany and Great Britain. Because of Ms. Syers, the first women's figure skating championship was held in 1906.[106]

• In 1912, Fanny Sperry Steele entered the Calgary Stampede bucking horse contest. Competing against men, she won first place — and she was the first woman to become the event's bucking horse champion. Wanting to show that her win wasn't a fluke, she entered the bucking horse contest again in 1913 — and again she won first place.[107]

Food

• While playing basketball at Auburn University, Charles Barkley weighed 300 pounds. Although he played basketball extremely well, Auburn fans and the fans of opposing teams thought that Mr. Barkley was fat, and they gave him such nicknames as the Round Mound of Rebound, Bread Truck, and Boy Gorge. Once, someone even sent a meal for Mr. Barkley to the Auburn bench during a game. His coach attempted to get Mr. Barkley to lose weight by having him run a mile with a pail of water in each hand and by having him run with heavy cinder blocks tied to his back, but he kept gaining weight. Eventually, after becoming a professional basketball player for the Philadelphia 76ers, Mr. Barkley decided to lose weight. He lost 10 pounds of fat through such dieting techniques as eating one pizza for supper instead of three.[108]

• The best gymnasts in the world are supposed to stay on healthy diets. At the ranch of world-class women's gymnastics coach Bela Karolyi, elite gymnasts eat chicken, rice, salad, and fruit, with no-fat salad dressing and no-fat milk. Once, Kerri Strug and Kim Zmeskal had to leave the ranch to get medical care, and instead of eating something like low-fat yoghurt for lunch, they ordered a deep-dish pizza and pigged out. As they were stuffing their faces, a local sportswriter they knew told them hello. They figured that the sportswriter would tell Mr. Karolyi that they were breaking training by eating pizza, but they found out later that the sportswriter had not. When Ms. Strug thanked the sportswriter for not telling on them, he replied, "Don't worry about it. Sportswriters train on pizza, too."[109]

• Dominique Moceanu was trained almost from infancy to be a world-class gymnast. The first time that she attended an out-of-state meet, the other gymnasts she trained with were surprised that she didn't know what salad dressing, bacon bits, and other high-fat food items were. Don't feel sorry for Dominique — her mother fed her such foods as homemade bread. Still, young Dominique sometimes went to other kids' houses to eat things that were not available in her own house. Once, she went to Becky Wildgen's house, whose mother had just made cupcakes. Becky says that Dominique "had like twelve of them."[110]

• Ice skating coach Frank Carroll once explained to a mischievous young skater named Christopher Bowman — at the request of the young boy's mother, who felt that Christopher was growing pudgy — the importance of a good, healthy diet. The very next day, Christopher's mother came to Mr. Carroll, bringing young Christopher with her — and the four boxes of doughnuts he had been eating. Mr. Carroll decided to teach the boy a lesson. He said, "Christopher, you sit down here. You are going to eat every one of those doughnuts before you get on the ice. And you're not moving from here until every one is gone."

After the boy had eaten the doughnuts, Mr. Carroll made him practice spins until finally young Christopher exited the ice and vomited.[111]

• In 1977, when she was 14 years old, tennis star Tracy Austin played Holland's Betty Stove in the quarterfinals of the United States Open. The older, bigger, heavier, and stronger Ms. Stove defeated her, then joked that young Tracy needed to drink more milk. Apparently, Tracy followed her advice. The following year, in the final match of a Stuttgart, West Germany, tournament, Tracy defeated Ms. Stove to win her first tournament as a professional tennis player.[112]

• A baseball player named Cletus Elwood (Boots) Poffenberger was once interviewed on a program sponsored by a cereal company. The interviewer tried to make Mr. Poffenberger give a free endorsement of the cereal by asking, "Now tell us, Boots, what is your favorite breakfast, taken with cream, sugar, and some sort of fruit?" But Boots, who would not allow himself to be manipulated, responded with, "Ham, eggs, and two bottles of beer."[113]

• In the old USSR, Soviet coaches had a problem. They wanted their athletes to eat caviar because of its high protein content; however, many athletes preferred to use the tins of caviar to barter for Western goods such as blue jeans. Russian ice skater Ekaterina Gordeeva writes that at the Calvary Olympics, the Soviet coaches solved the problem by opening each tin of caviar before giving it to the athletes.[114]

• When Czech tennis player Martina Navratilova first began touring in the United States, she fell in love with American fast food and gained 25 pounds in eight weeks. Other tennis players called her the "pancake champ," and when she returned home to Czechoslovakia, her father stopped calling his formerly skinny daughter by the nickname *Prut* ("Stick").[115]

Friends

• At the Nazi Olympics, held in Germany in 1936, Adolf Hitler hoped to demonstrate the superiority of the Aryan race. However, African-American track star Jesse Owens, representing the United

States, demolished that myth by winning four gold medals. A German athlete named Luz Long helped him to win one of the gold medals. To qualify for the long jump finals, Mr. Owens needed to make one of three attempts to jump a certain distance. Unfortunately, Mr. Owens committed faults on his two attempts. At this time, Mr. Long introduced himself to Mr. Owens and said, "You should be able to qualify with your eyes closed." Because Mr. Owens had faulted due to stepping on the take-off line instead of jumping before he reached it, Mr. Long put a towel on the ground a few inches before the take-off line, and Mr. Owens used that as the mark for his takeoff. On his third and final attempt, Mr. Owens qualified easily. The following day, Mr. Owens won the gold medal in the long jump, and Mr. Long won the silver medal. The two athletes, one black and one white, walked off arm in arm. Hitler was not pleased.[116]

• Chris Evert and Martina Navratilova fought fiercely but with affection on the tennis court. In one game, Chris hit a ball that struck Martina on the head. It knocked Martina down, but she quickly got up again and smiled. Chris even rubbed Martina's head when the two met again at the net. After Martina had defeated her, Chris said, "I can't believe it. I hit you in the head and you started playing better."[117]

Gambling

• Pittsburgh Phil Smith made millions of dollars from betting on the horses, partly because he bet on the great jockey Tod Sloan, who was ahead of his time. It was Mr. Sloan who learned that riding on the horse's neck made its gait freer and faster and who learned to let the other horses serve as wind breakers until the sprint at the end of the race. Mr. Sloan told Mr. Smith that he was bound to lose money betting on him no matter what horse he rode, but Mr. Smith replied, "Never mind that — look at the fun I have. If I lose on you today, I'll bet like hell on you tomorrow."[118]

• In 1961, before becoming a famous golfer, Lee Trevino worked at Hardy's Pitch-N-Putt, where he entertained people by hitting golf balls with a quart-sized soda bottle that he wrapped with tape. One day, a man offered to bet him that he couldn't use the bottle to hit a golf ball that would strike a 100-yard sign. Mr. Trevino asked, "What zero do you want me to hit?" The man decided not to bet.[119]

• Boxer Sugar Ray Robinson used to play golf with professional golfer Sam Snead. To even up the competition, Mr. Snead would spot Mr. Robinson one stroke per hole. Mr. Robinson once offered to return the favor if Mr. Snead ever wanted to box him — he would spot Mr. Snead the first five rounds of a six-round fight. Mr. Snead replied, "That's fine — as long as I can use my wedge."[120]

Gifts

• In 1996, comedian Elaine Boosler threw the first pitch at a Cleveland Indians game. Afterward, the Indians front office asked if they could do something for her. Ms. Boosler asked for a baseball signed by often-angry player Albert Belle, and they replied, "Wow, you really are a comedian." By the way, at the start of the 1992 baseball season, this sign was posted over Albert Belle's locker: "I'm going to be cool, calm, and collected this season. Yeah, right."[121]

• A boyfriend once gave All American Girls Professional Baseball League player Faye Dancer a diamond engagement ring. She said, "Why the heck are you giving me a ring?" — then she took the engagement ring to a jeweler, who removed the diamond and transferred it to her baseball ring.[122]

Good Deeds

• In 1989, the Detroit Public Schools ran out of money to fund its sports programs. One of the men who came to the rescue was Dave Bing, who had played professionally for the Detroit Pistons. He started to collect money from various sources — charities, Detroit businesses, and sports teams. In addition, the Pistons played a benefit game against a team of NBA All-Stars led by Magic Johnson. The $300,000 made by the benefit game added to the money Mr. Bing had already raised made a grand total of $600,000 — enough to run the Detroit Public Schools' sports teams! Why did Mr. Bing make such an effort to keep the sports teams going? He said, "Without them, I don't think some kids would be motivated to attend school."[123]

• At the 1964 Winter Olympic Games in Innsbruck, Austria, the British bobsled team of Anthony Nash and Robin Dixon had the lead after the first two runs but broke a bolt in their bobsled just before their third run. Bobsledder Eugenio Monti, who was competing for Italy, showed remarkably good sportsmanship by lending the Brits a bolt from his own bobsled. The loan kept the British team from dropping out of the competition and allowed them to win the gold medal. Mr. Monti had to wait until the 1968 Winter Olympic Games in Grenoble, France, to win the gold medal.[124]

• As a senior football player in high school, Barry Sanders, who later played professionally, rushed extremely well. In the last game of the season, his rushing helped put his team safely ahead of the other team, and he was taken out of the game to allow another player to compete. However, someone learned that Barry needed only 30 yards to become his league's leading rusher. Barry declined to go back into the game, reasoning that the game was already won and he should not rack up more yardage against a weaker team simply to win honor for himself.[125]

• Evonne Goolagong was born in a large family without much money in the town of Barellan, Australia. She showed great promise as a tennis player and had the opportunity to study with the great coach Victor Edwards in Sydney, 400 miles away, but her family didn't have the money to pay for her travel and city clothes. Fortunately, the people of Barellan took up a collection to pay her expenses. In 1971, Evonne won the women's championship at Wimbledon.[126]

• The world fell in love with Soviet gymnast Olga Korbut at the 1972 Olympic Games in Munich, Germany. Not only did she revolutionize gymnastics with high-difficulty and high-risk feats, she exhibited a winning personality to the audience. In the finals of the women's all-around competition, Olga fell off the uneven bars. As Olga was crying afterward, a woman in the audience jumped over a barrier, ran to her, and presented her with a bouquet of flowers.[127]

• Tennis star Billie Jean King needed money early in her career to go to Wimbledon — at the time tennis was regarded as a sport for amateurs, not professionals, and amateurs weren't allowed to make money. To raise the money for her to go to Wimbledon, the city of Long Beach, California, pitched in. Ms. King rewarded Long Beach with several Wimbledon championships, both in singles and in doubles.[128]

• When Barry Sanders was a junior in high school, his football coach asked if he wanted to play tailback, a position that would allow him to use his great speed. However, Barry declined, preferring to play wingback on offense and defensive back. Why? His brother was the starting tailback, and Barry did not want to compete against him for the position.[129]

• At the 1956 Olympics, Austrian skier Anton "Toni" Sailer almost did not get to skate in the downhill race. As he was tightening his bootstraps, one of them broke, and no one on his team had a replacement. In an act of remarkably good sportsmanship, an Italian team trainer gave Mr. Sailer a bootstrap. Mr. Sailer won the gold medal.[130]

Halloween

• One Halloween, basketball player Michael Jordan had to play an out-of-town game for the Chicago Bulls. Since he didn't want the neighborhood children to miss out on any Halloween candy, he put this sign on his apartment door: "Dear Kids, I'll Be Back In Three Days If You Want Trick Or Treat."[131]

Hitters

• Jay Kirke got hits in the major leagues until the opposing pitchers found out he couldn't hit a curve ball. After that, of course, he saw nothing but curve balls and was soon sent down into the minor leagues

— where he also saw nothing but curve balls. In one game, however, an opposing outfielder, who was intent on throwing out a man, made a wild throw — right at Mr. Kirke, who was waiting to bat. Mr. Kirke, instead of getting out of the way of the ball, swung his bat and hit the ball as hard as he could. Of course, the umpire ruled interference on the play. When Mr. Kirke's manager asked him what he had been thinking, he replied, "That's the first ball I've seen in months that didn't have a curve. I just couldn't resist hitting it."[132]

• Sometimes a major-league pitcher will get a little of his own back by throwing a knock-down pitch at a lesser hitter after the big bats have roughed him up. In one 1947 game, the New York Giants — a hard-hitting ball team — got three home runs in a row by Sid Gordon, Johnny Mize, and Walker Cooper. The next batter was Buddy Blattner — definitely not one of the big bats on his team. Mr. Blattner bit the dust twice on knock-down pitches, made his usual out, then returned to the dugout. Mr. Cooper said to him, "I'll say one thing, Blattner — they really respect you."[133]

• New York Yankee catcher Yogi Berra was a bad-ball hitter, meaning that he could connect with bad pitches and make a hit off them. Once, with two out in the bottom half of the ninth, two runners on base, and the Yankees behind by two runs, Mr. Berra hit a pitch that was close to his ankles for a game-winning three-run home run. When the losing pitcher was asked if he knew of a way to get Mr. Berra out, he replied, "Yeah. With a pistol."[134]

• When the New York Yankees were playing in Chicago, the game was tied in extra innings and Yankee traveling secretary Mark Roth worried about whether the game would end in time for the team to catch the train. Babe Ruth heard Mr. Roth expressing his worries, and he told him, "Don't worry, Mark. We'll make that train. I'll fix that." Going up to bat a few minutes later, Babe hit a game-winning home run. The Yankees caught the train.[135]

• As a bad-ball hitter, Yogi Berra would swing at bad balls and get hits off them. While he was playing Triple A baseball with the Newark Bears in 1946, his manager tried to get him to stop swinging at baseballs not in the strike zone. The manager said, "Yogi, next time you're up, think about what you're doing." After striking out in three pitches, Mr. Berra decided, "You can't hit and think at the same time."[136]

• "Shoeless Joe" Jackson claimed to have hit the world's longest home run. According to Mr. Jackson, he hit a home run out of a baseball park in his native South Carolina. The baseball landed in a Southern Railroad rail car that was traveling by the ballpark. Later, the baseball was found in the rail car in Washington D.C. — 500 miles away from where Mr. Jackson had hit it.[137]

• Hank Aaron came up to bat in the 1957 World Series, and the opposing catcher, Yogi Berra, told him, "You got the bat facing the wrong way. Turn it around so you can see the trademark." Mr. Aaron replied, "Didn't come up here to read. Came up here to hit."[138]

Horse Racing

• In 1936 in Cuba, American track star Jesse Owens was supposed to run an exhibition race against Conrado Rodrigues, but the Amateur Athletic Union (AAU), which was angry at Mr. Owens because he had skipped some money-raising exhibitions after the 1936 Olympics (although Mr. Owens would not have been paid for running in the exhibitions), threatened to revoke Mr. Rodrigues' amateur status. Therefore, instead of racing against Mr. Rodrigues, Mr. Owens raced against a horse! Because he was given a big lead, Mr. Owens won.[139]

• The owner of a horse once gave famed jockey Eddie Arcaro detailed instructions on how to win a race. Mr. Arcaro followed the instructions exactly, but he finished last instead of first. The horse's owner was angry and said to him, "I told you exactly what to do! You were supposed to stay in fourth position until the last turn and then take the lead as you came into the stretch." Mr. Arcaro replied, "What? And leave the horse?"[140]

Injuries

• After gymnast Kurt Thomas won a gold medal in floor exercise at the 1978 World Championships — thus winning the United States its first gold medal ever at this level — he became an instant celebrity and even appeared on *The Tonight Show with Johnny Carson*. During his appearance, Johnny asked him, "Kurt, have you ever had any injuries in gymnastics?" Mr. Thomas replied, "Nothing serious, although I did fracture my neck once."[141]

• Dana X. Bible was a football coach at the University of Texas. He cared about his players, and he once had a center who would play hurt, hiding his injury so he wouldn't be taken out of the game. Therefore, Mr. Bible asked another player to keep an eye on the center, and if the player noticed that the center was hurt to tell him so that he could take the center out of the game.[142]

• Rodeo clown Benjie Prudom once found herself in a tight spot with a bull in an arena. She put her hand out in front of her, and the 1,900-pound bull ran into it. Of course, people were concerned about her, and when she had gotten out of the arena, someone asked if her hand was broken. She replied, "No, but my fingernail is."[143]

Language

• World-class women's gymnastics coaches Bela Karolyi and his wife, Marta, used to speak in their native Romanian when discussing the faults their gymnasts had made during practice. However, they noticed something odd after the young gymnast Betty Okino began training with them. When they used Romanian to criticize an error in a gymnast's routine, the next time the gymnast did that routine, the error had been corrected. One day, Bela mentioned, in Romanian, an error that young Betty had made and Betty's eyes grew round. Bela noticed, and he asked her, "You speak Romanian, don't you?" Betty whispered,

"Yes," everyone laughed, and thereafter Bela and Marta communicated in Hungarian.[144]

• When world-class gymnastics coach Bela Karolyi defected from Romania to the United States, he didn't know English. He started work cleaning in a restaurant for a man who called him a son of a bitch. Since Mr. Karolyi didn't know what the words meant, he looked them up in a Romanian-English dictionary. "Son" meant "child of," and "bitch" meant "female dog," so Mr. Karolyi put the meanings together, and since everybody loves little puppy dogs, he figured the restaurant owner liked him and was calling him something good. It wasn't until later, when Mr. Karolyi called one of his gymnastics students a son of a bitch, that he learned that the phrase was not complimentary.[145]

• Maury Maverick, Jr. was raised to be polite and not use bad language in letters. While he was a student at the school that became the Texas Military Institute, he felt that he should have received a letter in football. When he wrote home that he did not receive it, he wrote that he had been "sexually intercoursed" concerning the letter in football.[146]

• Dominique Moceanu won a gold medal as a member of the United States women's gymnastics team in 1996 at the Olympic Games in Atlanta, Georgia. Her mother, Camelia, was born in Romania and came to the U.S. as an adult. Camelia learned English by watching television and looking up words she didn't know in her Romanian-English dictionary.[147]

• A boxer named Young Griffo hung out at a billiard parlor owned by New York Giants manager John McGraw and jockey Tod Sloan, where he was in the habit of asking everybody for loans. Once, he met an Englishman and asked for the loan of a buck. The Englishman asked, "How much is a buck?" Young Griffo replied, "Twenty dollars."[148]

• After retiring from pitching, Dizzy Dean became an announcer, despite his lack of knowledge of English grammar. Once he was accused of ruining the syntax of his young listeners. Mr. Dean asked, "Sin tax? What will those fellers in Washington think of next?"[149]

Chapter 4: From Managers to Olympics

Managers

• Casey Stengel used to try to get games called on account of darkness when his team was ahead late in a game. Often, he would light matches in the dugout as a hint to umpires that it was getting dark. In one game, his team was ahead, darkness was coming, but his pitcher was starting to tire. Mr. Stengel made several trips to the mound in an attempt to stall and force the umpires to call the game, but the umpires were wise to him and determined to give the other team a full inning. Finally, Mr. Stengel walked out to the mound — using a flashlight to light his way. The fans laughed, but the umpires threw him out of the game.[150]

• Casey Stengel was managing the Brooklyn Dodgers when he decided to pull pitcher "Boom Boom" Beck. After a lengthy conference on the mound, during which Boom Boom protested against being pulled, Boom Boom angrily turned around and tried to throw the baseball over the right-field fence. The baseball didn't quite make it and hit the fence. Dodger right fielder Hank Wilson had been daydreaming, and when he heard the baseball hit the fence, he thought play had resumed. Hank fielded the baseball, then threw it to second base to cut off the nonexistent runner.[151]

• During his early days in show business, comedian Joe E. Brown had a chance to play for a baseball club. Because the club was just starting, he saw no reason not to ask for his favorite position, so he told the club manager he wanted to play second base and would not play shortstop or third base. This made the manager laugh because — as he pointed out to Mr. Brown — not only was he was the manager, but he also played second base.[152]

Martial Arts

• Tajima wanted to achieve the highest level of skill in the martial arts. To achieve his goal, he sought a teacher, eventually choosing

Kanjin, who reluctantly accepted him as a student, then put him to work doing the menial labor of a servant. For a long time, nothing happened, then as Tajima was gathering firewood, a blow from a stick crashed on his head. Looking behind him, Tajima saw his teacher, Kanjin. From then on, Kanjin made Tajima's life miserable. Tajima never knew when his teacher would sneak up behind him and hit him with a stick. One day, Tajima saw his teacher bent over a pot, cooking rice. Thinking that this was the perfect opportunity for revenge, Tajima grabbed the teacher's stick, snuck up behind Kanjin, then tried to hit him with as much force as he could. However, Kanjin whirled around and stopped the blow with the lid of the cooking pot. Tajima bowed to his teacher, then continued his studies. Eventually, Tajima learned to be constantly alert against surprise attacks.[153]

• In the 1960s British tongue-in-cheek TV series *The Avengers*, Mrs. Cathy Gale, played by Honor Blackman, used judo to subdue her attackers. The use of judo came about through a process of elimination. The producers had already rejected the idea of Mrs. Gale screaming for help. At first, they had her reach into a handbag for a gun, but that grew tiresome. Then they tried having Mrs. Gale wear a gun in a garter holster, but it made her walk bowlegged. Next they tried concealing the gun in an under-arm holster, but tight sweaters are incompatible with concealed guns. Then came concealed daggers and short swords, but they kept cutting her bra straps. Finally, René Burdet, who had been the head of the Resistance in Marseilles during World War II, taught Ms. Blackman how to throw people. Later, both Ms. Blackman and Patrick Macnee, who played John Steed, learned judo from Douglas Robinson, a 9th Dan black belt.[154]

• It is easy to be intimidated by people without the power to harm you. Martial arts expert and actor Bruce Lee noticed that this sometimes happened to martial arts student Joe Hyams, so he drew a chalk circle on a driveway, then had Mr. Hyams stand inside the circle. Outside the circle, Mr. Lee made a few martial arts moves. Mr. Hyams stiffened, but Mr. Lee told him he had no reason for fear because as long as Mr. Lee was outside the circle, he wasn't close enough to harm him. Mr. Lee drew a little closer, and again Mr. Hyams stiffened. Again, Mr. Lee pointed out that he wasn't close enough to do him any harm. Mr. Lee then jumped inside the circle, and Mr. Hyams moved back. "Good," said Mr. Lee. "You've moved your circle back so that I am no threat to you." This exercise taught Mr. Hyams to recognize when he was truly threatened and not to worry about mere attempts at intimidation.[155]

Media

• The 1965 Figure Skating World Championships took place in Colorado Springs, Colorado. Back then, figure skating was not recognized as a major sport, and incredibly, only eight accredited media people were present. Although you would expect the figure skaters to do their best to please the media, the head of the Canadian delegation tried to deny them access to Petra Burka after she won her gold medal. Eventually, they managed to speak to her but only for approximately 90 seconds. Following this debacle, figure skater Donald Knight lunched with media representatives Frank Orr and George Gross. Mr. Gross was aggrieved with the process of trying to interview Ms. Burka after her win, so Mr. Knight volunteered to give them his interview right then. He gave the reporters quotes to use if he finished third, as expected; if he got lucky and finished second; if he got really lucky and won the gold medal; and if he messed up and did not win a medal. In other words, Mr. Orr and Mr. Gross had their quotes from Mr. Knight before his event even started. Mr. Orr says, "Ever since then, Don Knight has been one of my favorite athletes." (Mr. Knight won the bronze medal, as expected.)[156]

• In 1989, figure skating choreographer Sandra Bezic worked on the full-length motion picture *Carmen on Ice*, where she had some interesting experiences. For one thing, a German actor who played the role of the officer who orders Carmen's arrest had stated on his resume that he could skate — he lied. For filming, other people had to push him into the scene with just enough force so that he would stop where he was supposed to. For one scene, Katerina Witt, who played Carmen, was supposed to land a triple jump at 4 a.m. She missed the jump 30 times in a row due to exhaustion and rough ice on a smaller-than-normal rink, then she rubbed the bald spot of Ms. Bezic's husband for good luck. After successfully landing the jump, Ms. Witt said that she had discovered a good-luck charm.[157]

• In Maryland in 1973, Ilie Nastase and Clark Graebner played an Indoor Tennis match at which a *Washington Post* reporter sat courtside typing in order to write his story and file it by his deadline. The tennis players complained about the noise made by the typewriter, and the tennis fans told the reporter to stop his noisy typing because it distracted the players. However, because of his deadline, the reporter ignored the fans. Eventually, a fan grew so annoyed that he grabbed the reporter's typewriter and ran away with it.[158]

• John Chapman, drama critic for the *New York Daily News*, loved Shakespeare. He once started to attend a new production of *Henry V* at the Shakespeare theater at Stratford, Connecticut, but was surprised to see gymnasts performing on stage. Thinking that he was early for the play, he asked an usher what was being performed on stage, and he was surprised when the usher told him that the performance was *Henry V* and that it opened with gymnasts. Mr. Chapman replied, "The hell it does," and then he left the theater.[159]

• Jack Murphy, a sportswriter for the *San Diego Union*, was assigned to cover the Rose Bowl, but he decided to first do some skiing in the mountains above Lake Arrowhead. He had a grand time and waited until the last minute before heading to the Rose Bowl. Fortunately, he was able to drive fast and — despite a snowstorm — make it to the Rose Bowl in time to cover it. However, he startled many football fans who stood in the warm sun and stared at Mr. Murphy's car, which was covered with snow and ice.[160]

• *The New York Times* hired its first woman sports editor in the late 1970s, and women's sports began to get considerably more coverage than when the *Times* had a male sports editor. On June 1, 1980, this headline appeared in the *Times*: "Massachusetts Woman Takes Weight-Lifting Title." The article reported that Leslie Sewall had won the 114-pound national AAU title. Unfortunately, the headline had gotten one thing wrong — Leslie Sewall is a man.[161]

• Olga Korbut astonished the world at the 1972 Olympic Games in Munich with her revolutionary and high-risk gymnastics feats. As she performed a back somersault and recatch on the uneven bars, news commentator George Madux could say only, "Oh! My! Wow!" When he was asked if Olga's feat had ever been accomplished before, he replied, "Not by any human."[162]

• Ice dancers Jayne Torvill and Christopher Dean received over 100 perfect 6's in their career, but their first perfect 6 came in the 1979 British championships and was given to them by an octogenarian named Molly Phillips, who was rumored to give perfect 6's so that her face would appear on TV.[163]

• In a column he wrote for *Catholic New York*, Cardinal John O'Connor criticized the playing of professional baseball games on Sunday. The *New York Post* covered the controversy in an article headlined "Sermon on the Mound."[164]

• Chess world champion Gary Kasparov has an interesting way of dealing with reporters he doesn't want to talk to — he ignores them. Eventually, the reporters go away.[165]

Mishaps

• Some members of Charlie Barnet's jazz band decided to go swimming in San Francisco on a very hot day, so they plugged the cracks under the doors of their hotel room, turned on the water full force in the bathtub and let the water overflow. Eventually, they had a foot and a half or two feet of water on the floor, and they had a grand time "swimming" until the water leaked through the floor into the hotel room below. The hotel management, of course, was upset and brought in Mr. Barnet to see the damage. Mr. Barnet was also upset, and after calling his band members a few unprintable names, said, "The least you could have done was invite me."[166]

• Years ago, sportscasters Chris Schenkel, Bud Wilkerson, and O.J. Simpson were on TV commenting on the Hula Bowl, which is played in Hawaii. At a pause in the game, a TV camera showed a young lady, and Mr. Schenkel asked, "Bud, isn't that the young lady who gave us a lei before the game?"[167]

Money

• When professional baseball teams started to pay for the wives of All-Stars to attend the All-Star game, the single All-Stars complained, and so they were allowed to bring along a parent, sibling, or friend at the team's expense. In 1984, Damaso Garcia was an All-Star, and he asked his friend Alfredo Griffin, an infielder, to go with him. When they arrived at the All-Star game, they discovered that infielder Alan Trammel had been hurt, and Mr. Griffin, since he was already there, was asked to take his place. Ironically, Mr. Griffin could never become an All-Star on his own merits, but he had an incentive clause in his contract saying he would receive a $25,000 bonus if he became an All-Star. Since he indisputably was on an All-Star team, he received his $25,000.[168]

• Willie Johnson, a caddie of the Royal and Ancient Golf Club at St. Andrews in Scotland, got his nickname of "Trap Door" because of how he used to make extra income. Claiming that one leg was shorter than the other, he had a special boot made with a hollow sole and a metal door. Inside the sole he used to trap the "lost" golf balls of the people he caddied for. His special boot could hold up to six "lost" balls, which he would resell for extra income.[169]

• Competitive figure skating can be expensive. In 1995, Rudy Galindo retired from competitive figure skating because he didn't have enough money to pay for training. However, the 1996 United States

Championships were being held in his hometown of San Jose, California, so he entered. Smart move. Despite being an underdog, he won the gold medal and became THE story of the championships. His victory led to a career as a professional figure skater and lots of money for training.[170]

• Figure skater Gary Beacom once felt that judge Kathy Casey had given him an unfairly low score at a competition, so he publicly skated over to her and handed her a dollar the next time he skated. He was satisfied with the result of his "bribe" — she gave him a higher score than she had the first time. Mr. Beacom joked, "It does seem possible to bribe the judges, even in broad daylight."[171]

• Figure skater Rosalynn Sumners had a tendency to put on weight. When she was skating for Disney, her contract required her to be weighed each week, and if she was three pounds over a certain weight, Disney fined her $10. After a while, Ms. Sumners began to stand on the scales each week with a $10 bill in her hand.[172]

• Being a competitive figure skater can be expensive. Until 1995, Michelle Kwan wore only used skates, partly because they were more comfortable and partly because they were cheaper. In fact, her father sold their house and moved his family in with Michelle's grandparents so he could raise money for her training.[173]

• Winning a championship in the modern Olympic Games means a great deal, and it meant a great deal in the ancient world. For example, for the rest of their lives ancient Olympic champions did not have to pay taxes![174]

Mothers

• When Carol Heiss was a little girl, her ice skating teacher urged her parents to hire a professional coach for her. However, coaching is expensive, and Mr. Heiss' salary was enough only to support his family. Nevertheless, Mr. and Mrs. Heiss asked the teacher how good their daughter could be with the best coaching. The teacher replied, "We believe that if she studies hard, in ten years she can be the champion of the world." Immediately, Mrs. Heiss began working at a part-time job. Carol did study hard, and Mrs. Heiss saw Carol win her first world championship. (Carol went on to win four more world championships.) Unfortunately, Mrs. Heiss died of cancer shortly before Carol won a gold medal at the 1960 Olympics. When the medal was given to Carol, she whispered, "It's for you, Mother. I promised."[175]

• Tiger Woods' mother, Kultida, wanted her son to grow up to be a good sportsman. She once made Tiger watch tennis brat John McEnroe on television. When Mr. McEnroe argued a call that an official had made, she told Tiger, "See that? Never that! I don't like that. I will not have my reputation as a parent ruined by that." At a golf tournament, Tiger hit a bad shot and angrily hit his golf bag with his club. His mother immediately reported him to the tournament director and demanded that he be penalized two strokes. When Tiger complained, she said, "Who made the bad shot? Whose fault? You want to hit something? Hit yourself in the head!"[176]

• When world-class figure skater Tiffany Chin was eight years old, she received a gift from her mother — her very first pair of skates, which cost $1 at a garage sale. Tiffany was very happy to receive the slightly used skates, but of course, she didn't look like a world-class figure skater her first time on the ice. Instead, she did what everyone does the first time they try to skate — she fell down. Later, of course, she improved dramatically. In 1985, she was the United States Ladies National Champion, and in 1985 and 1986, she was the World Bronze Medalist.[177]

• In 1986, Lyn St. James was involved in a crash while racing in California at the Riverside International Raceway. Her car was bumped by another car, then her car sped out of control and several other cars hit it. As her car burst into flames, Ms. St. James crawled out, then walked to a telephone. The race was being televised, and she knew her mother would be worried about her, so she called immediately to say that she was all right.[178]

Motivation

• Gymnastics coach Bela Karolyi understands how to motivate gymnasts. At his gymnastics training camp in Houston, Texas, there were three gyms. Two were tan, and one was blue. The tan gyms were for ordinary gymnasts, while the blue gym was for the elite gymnasts who compete in the National Championships, the World Championships, and the Olympics. All the young gymnasts who trained with Mr. Karolyi hoped someday to train in the blue gym.[179]

• Figure skating coach Gustave Lussi was a master of motivation. He coached Dorothy Hamill when she was very young, and each time she learned a new jump, he rewarded her with coins. After long hours of training, young Dorothy managed to land both the double lutz and the double flip at the same practice session. She took the coins, framed them, and hung them on her wall.[180]

• Back when figure skater Tiffany Chin was competing, she had little trouble motivating herself to practice. She figured that the choice was between not practicing and falling down in front of an audience, or practicing and not falling down in front of an audience. She strongly preferred to practice in private and not fall down in public.[181]

• Gymnasts have different ways of motivating themselves to perform well. Olympic gold medalist Dominique Dawes writes the words "Determination," "Dedication," and "Dynamics" on her bathroom mirror to motivate herself before meets. These words make up what she calls her "3-D philosophy" of competition.[182]

• Soviet gymnastics champion Ludmilla Tourischeva used to mark the days of the World Championships on her calendar — and on each day she would mark "VICTORY!"[183]

Names

• In 1976, the Atlanta Braves began to print each player's nickname above his number on his uniform. Andy Messersmith wore No. 17, which was the number of the channel broadcasting the programs of WTCH, a television station owned by Ted Turner, who also owned the Braves. Because Mr. Messersmith didn't have a nickname, Mr. Turner decided to put "Channel" above the 17 on Mr. Messersmith's uniform. Unfortunately, the National League President didn't like the joke, regarding it as advertising, so he forced the Braves to remove "Channel" from Mr. Messersmith's uniform.[184]

• Golfer Tiger Woods' real first name is Eldrick, which was specially chosen by his parents, Earl and Kultida Woods. His mother says that she and her husband took the first letters of their first names and put them at the beginning and end of Tiger's real first name in order "to show that no matter what, we will always be at your side." Where did the nickname "Tiger" come from? Tiger was given his nickname by his Vietnam War veteran father, who wished to honor a South Vietnamese soldier who had saved him from being killed by a sniper.[185]

• Jair Lynch says that he became a successful gymnast — he is the first black gymnast to win an Olympic medal and only the second black gymnast to compete at the Games — because of his name. In Senegalese, Jair means "one who sees the light." According to Jair Lynch, "Joe" Lynch would not have become successful.[186]

• Ice skater Dorothy Hamill is nearsighted, and in her competitive days she wore oversized glasses to help her see well enough to do such school figures, aka compulsory figures, as a figure eight. Because of her poor eyesight, her fellow performers in the Ice Capades nicknamed her "Squint."[187]

• In 1996, Jaycie Phelps won Olympics gold as a member of the United States "Magnificent Seven" women's gymnastics team at the Atlanta Games. Her parents are Jack and Cheryl Phelps, and Jaycie got her name from the initials of her parents' first names.[188]

• Former heavyweight champion Mike Tyson has a lisp and so, when he was growing up, other children called him "Fairy Boy."[189]

Olympics

• At the 1984 Olympic Games in Los Angeles, gymnast Bart Conner attended the opening ceremonies, where he saw thousands of people smiling and waving flags. After the Olympics, he received a letter from a young girl, who asked, "Did you see me that day in the Los Angeles Coliseum? I was the one smiling and waving the flag." Mr. Conner says that in fact he did see her: "If only for an instant, I actually did feel and 'see' every face." In addition, looking around at the thousands of people in the Coliseum, Mr. Conner said to fellow gymnast Jim Hartung, "Wouldn't it be great to spot somebody you knew in this mob?" At that moment, Mr. Hartung said, "Bart, look. There's your mom." Mr. Conner did look, and he saw his parents in the crowd.[190]

• On April 10, 1896, a Greek named Spyridon Louis won the marathon race at the Olympics held in Greece. He had trained by running after his mule as he carried water from village to village. After winning, he became famous, but he declined to take advantage of his celebrity even though his fellow Greeks offered him such things as free dinners and free haircuts. However, when King George I of Greece asked if there was anything he would like to have as a reward for winning the marathon, he replied, "Yes, please, a cart and a horse so I won't have to run after my mule any more."[191]

• Winning an Olympic gold medal can be exhausting, both physically and mentally. After winning her gold medal in women's figure skating at the 1998 Games in Nagano, Japan, Tara Lipinski fell asleep so soundly that the next morning, Megan Faulkner was able to braid her hair without waking her. In fact, Tara was so soundly asleep that she slept through a moderate earthquake. When a reporter asked her what she thought about the earthquake, Tara replied, "What earthquake?"[192]

• The life of a world-class gymnastics coach may not be what you think it is. At the 1984 Olympic Games in Los Angeles, Mary Lou

Retton, who was born in West Virginia but was coached by Bela Karolyi in Houston, Texas, won the gold medal in the all-around. Mr. Karolyi, however, was not the coach of the United States team, so he was not given a pass into the Olympic Village. For part of the Olympics, he slept in the hotel room of a friend, but once his friend left LA, he slept in a car.[193]

• The finals in the broad jump at the 1936 Olympic Games in Berlin, Germany, featured a fierce competition between the American Jesse Owens and the German Luz Long. During the finals, they tied the Olympic record once and beat the record five times, but when the contest was over, Mr. Owens held both the new Olympic record and a gold medal. In defeat, Mr. Long was a good sportsman. He congratulated Mr. Owens, and the two athletes became friends.[194]

• After ice skater Peggy Fleming won her gold medal at the 1968 Olympic Games, she was given both her medal and a kiss by Avery Brundage, the aged chair of the International Olympic Committee, who was vigilant in making sure that the athletes participating in the Olympics were amateurs. After Ms. Fleming got her medal and kiss, reporters asked her what Mr. Brundage was like as a kisser. She replied, "He was an amateur."[195]

• At the 1976 Olympic Games in Montreal, John Walker, the 1,500-meter track champion from New Zealand, drank a few beers in order to come up with enough urine for his mandatory drug test following his gold medal-winning performance. Finally succeeding in his objective, he held the bottle up and said, "I'm very proud of this. It was harder than running the race."[196]

• At the 1912 Olympic Games, Jim Thorpe won gold medals in the pentathlon and decathlon events. At the awards ceremony, King Gustav V of Sweden told him, "You, sir, are the greatest athlete in the world." Mr. Thorpe replied, "Thanks, King."[197]

Chapter 5: From People with Handicaps to War

People with Handicaps

• Cordell Brown, who has cerebral palsy, is the founder of Echoing Hills Village, Inc., a non-profit organization that runs a summer camp and residences for adults with handicaps. He became a lifelong fan of football, in part because several Cleveland Browns players in training camp played with him and other children with handicaps while he was receiving treatment at Bowling Green University. Later, Mr. Brown became manager of his high school team, but because of his cerebral palsy, which made him uncoordinated, it was quite an experience for him to carry water to the team during a time out. Frequently, he arrived completely soaked and with no water at all left in the bucket.[198]

• Doctors can't explain why Carol Johnston was born with only one arm, but she didn't let it stop her from becoming an All-American gymnast. Called "Lefty," Ms. Johnston won silver medals on balance beam and floor exercise at the 1978 United States national gymnastics championships in Seattle, Washington. (She was almost late for her performance on the beam, because she was eating chocolate ice cream.) Ms. Johnston said, "I'm not supposed to be a gymnast physically, but no one told me that mentally. No one said I couldn't be creative with one arm." So she became creative with one arm — creative enough to become a famous gymnast.[199]

• On August 19, 1951, Bill Veeck pulled a notable publicity stunt for his baseball team, the St. Louis Browns. He hired a little person — formerly known as a midget — to bat for his team. The little person wore a uniform that belonged to the seven-year-old son of a team vice president, and he used a toy bat. Because of his tiny strike zone, the little person walked in four pitches, and a real baseball player was sent in to run for him. On his uniform, the little person wore the smallest number ever given to a professional baseball player: 1/8.[200]

• Congressman Morris K. Udall had a glass eye, the result of an accident and a botched operation when he was a child. In college, he played center in basketball and during one game, he played extremely well, scoring 24 points. When he came out of the game, a sportswriter who came from the town of the opposing team told him, "Udall, you are a liar. No one shoots like that with a glass eye." Mr. Udall took his glass eye out of its socket and handed it to the sportswriter, saying, "Mister, I haven't been able to see much out of this one — you try it."[201]

• Kitty O'Neil, a stunt woman on TV's *Wonder Woman* series, broke the land speed record for women on December 6, 1976, in the Alvord Desert in Oregon. She drove a rocket car named the Motivator, breaking the old record of 308 miles an hour by over 200 miles per hour — her new record was almost 513 miles an hour. After she finished her historic drive, she climbed out of the Motivator to the cheers of the crowd. However, Ms. O'Neil didn't hear the cheers — she is deaf.[202]

• Central Ohio TV sportscaster Jimmy Crum once covered a bowling tournament for children who are handicapped mentally or physically. One small girl with Down's syndrome kept trying to get the bowling ball down the lane, but ball after ball went into the gutter. Finally, one bowling ball went straight down the center of the lane — and the girl was ecstatic. Mr. Crum congratulated the girl, and she put her arms around his neck, hugged him, and said, "I love you, Mr. Man."[203]

• At the 1992 Olympic Games held in Barcelona, Spain, Jackie Joyner-Kersee won a gold medal in the heptathlon. However, after she clinched heptathlon gold in the 800-meter race, she was forced to delay her victory lap because an asthma attack made it difficult for her to breathe. Fans chanted her name, and finally she was able to take her victory lap and shake hands with some of her fans.[204]

Pitchers

• George Jessel lived long and prospered, being born in 1898 and dying in 1981, with many years of fame, fortune, and divorces in the middle. In 1910, he was batboy for the New York Giants, managed by John McGraw, at the Polo Grounds. At this time, the big stars were Ty Cobb and, near the end of his career, Rube Waddell. Mr. Jessel used to tell the story of Mr. Waddell being called to pitch with the opposing team having three men on base and no outs. Mr. Waddell made his outfielders come in and sit on the bench, then he struck out the next three batters.[205]

• When pitcher Greg Maddux first reported to the Chicago Cubs, he was very young and he looked small in comparison to many major leaguers. One of the Cubs coaches, John Vokovich, asked team manager Gene Michael, "Aren't you going to say hello to your new pitcher?" Mr. Michael looked around, saw Mr. Maddux, and said, "That's the batboy." Mr. Maddux ended up becoming the first person ever to win the Cy Young Award four years in a row.[206]

• In 1934, brothers Dizzy Dean and Daffy Dean pitched a double-header for the St. Louis Cardinals. Dizzy had a no-hitter until the 9th inning, when he gave up three hits but still won the game. Daffy, however, pitched brilliantly for the entire game and earned a no-hitter. After the game, Dizzy congratulated Daffy and said, "Why didn't you tell me you were going to pitch a no-hitter? Then I would have pitched one, too."[207]

• New York Yankees rookie pitcher Henry Johnson was just starting to eat a sandwich in the bullpen when he was called up to pitch relief against the Philadelphia Athletics. He asked, "Who's coming up to bat for the A's?" The answer came back — three power hitters: "Cochrane, Simmons, and Foxx." Mr. Johnson put down his sandwich and said, "Don't let anybody touch that. I'll be right back."[208]

• Former major league pitcher Johnny Sain once faced the great hitter Rogers Hornsby. Mr. Sain threw a pitch, which was ruled a ball by the umpire. Then he threw another pitch, which was also ruled a ball. Annoyed, Mr. Sain walked halfway to the umpire and said sarcastically, "Will you let know when I pitch a strike?" The umpire replied, "When you pitch a strike, Mr. Hornsby will let you know."[209]

• Joe Garagiola once was catching for a young pitcher who was facing the great hitter Stan Musial. Mr. Garagiola kept giving signs for pitches, but the pitcher kept shaking them off. Finally, Mr. Garagiola went to the pitcher's mound and asked the young pitcher what he wanted to throw against Mr. Musial. "Nothing," the pitcher replied. "I want to hold the ball as long as possible."[210]

• The great hitter Stan Musial once faced pitcher "Bobo" Newsome and hit a single, a triple, and a home run. The fourth time Mr. Musial was set to hit against Mr. Newsome, Mr. Newsome's manager decided to send in a rookie pitcher. The rookie pitcher took the ball from Mr. Newsome and asked if Mr. Musial had any weaknesses. "Yeah," replied Mr. Newsome, "he can't hit doubles."[211]

Practical Jokes

• While attending Syracuse University, Dave Bing roomed with Frank Nicoletti. Mr. Bing is African American, while Mr. Nicoletti is white. Both enjoyed playing practical jokes on the other. Sometimes, Mr. Nicoletti would be in the dorm hall late at night when suddenly Mr. Bing would open the door to their room and roll some cans down the hall. Mr. Nicoletti would immediately run for their room to try to escape being blamed for the noise, but the resident assistant would come running to investigate the noise and see Mr. Nicoletti going into his room. The resident assistant would then enter the room, see Mr. Bing innocently kneeling and saying his prayers, turn to Mr. Nicoletti, and put him on probation. However, Mr. Nicoletti also played practical jokes on Mr. Bing. Because Mr. Bing was involved with Reserve Officers' Training Corps, he had to get up early to do ROTC drills.

Mr. Nicoletti would change the time on Mr. Bing's alarm clock so that Mr. Bing would think that he was getting up at 7 a.m. when it was actually 5 a.m. Sometimes, when Mr. Bing went outside on a bitterly cold morning for ROTC drills, he would discover that he was the only person up. Then he would look at his wristwatch and discover that his roommate had fooled him again.[212]

• Ice skaters Peggy Fleming and Robin Cousins are practical jokers who tried to break up each other while performing together on the ice. For one performance, Ms. Fleming wrote this message on her eyelids for Mr. Cousins to read as they were skating in public together: "BITE ME." Mr. Cousins quickly got revenge. Ms. Fleming had to make a quick costume change, slipping on a coat then returning immediately to the show and skating. When she did so, she discovered that Mr. Cousins had altered the coat — padding made Ms. Fleming's breasts appear to be humongous.[213]

• Kelly McCormick won silver and bronze medals in the Olympics in the 1980s as a springboard diver. While training at the Ohio State University, she was coached by Vince Panzanno. As a joke on him, she and the other divers on the team colored their hair bright pink, but the joke fell flat. Later, they discovered why — Mr. Panzanno is colorblind.[214]

Practice

• Jim Thorpe wanted to play football at the Carlisle Indian School, so one day he dressed in a football uniform that was too big for him and begged Coach Glenn Scobey "Pop" Warner to give him a chance. Pop Warner finally told him to give the first team some tackling practice. Therefore, Mr. Thorpe was given a football and told to run against the first team so they could tackle him. Mr. Thorpe did run — through the first-team players and into the end zone. Pop Warner said, "You're supposed to give the first team some tackling practice, not run through them!" Mr. Thorpe replied, "Nobody tackles Jim" — then he ran through the first-team players and into the end zone again. Pop Warner got Mr. Thorpe a uniform that fit, and soon Mr. Thorpe became an All-American football player.[215]

• When United States gymnast Hollie Vise was 12 years old, she told her mother, "When I was young, I always wanted to be in the Olympics." By the way, Ms. Vise is a serious gymnast. She even has a balance beam (one that is low to the floor) in her parents' dining room.[216]

• Babe Didrikson won a record 17 golf tournaments in a row. How did she do it? She often hit 1,500 golf balls a day and practiced until her hands were blistered and bleeding.[217]

Prayer

• At the 1996 Olympics Games held in Atlanta, Kerri Strug was the last member of the United States women's gymnastics team to perform on their final apparatus: the vault. On her first performance, she vaulted badly and injured her ankle, but she summoned her strength and vaulted again. Before the second vault, she said this prayer: "Please, God, help me out here. I'm just asking you once here. I've always tried to be a good person. I've always tried to do what's right. Please, just let me do this vault." Her second vault was good, and the U.S. women won the gold medal in team competition.[218]

• After young professional tennis player Tracy Austin was sidelined with an inflamed sciatica nerve in early 1981, she was forced to rest, although she was very eager to start playing competitively again. Therefore, she used to say this prayer: "God, give me patience — but hurry up!"[219]

Prejudice

• When Jackie Robinson became the first black baseball player to compete on a major league team, the Brooklyn Dodgers, he was often heckled by opposing players. Ben Chapman, the team manager of the Philadelphia Phillies, ordered his players to heckle Mr. Robinson during some games early in the season, so they kept up a relentless torrent of racist abuse directed against him. Although Mr. Robinson was tempted to fight, he knew that a fight would set back integration in the major leagues. For a few games, the other Dodgers stayed silent, but finally Dodger second baseman Eddie Stanky, a Southerner, yelled at the Phillies, "Listen, you yellow-bellied cowards, why don't you yell at somebody who can answer back?" After that, other Dodgers started defending Mr. Robinson, and Mr. Robinson became accepted as a member of the team.[220]

• For decades, large areas of the Indianapolis 500 grounds were for men only. For example, women — even women owners of Indianapolis 500 racing cars — were not allowed in the Indianapolis 500 garages. In 1950, racing fans were outraged when the movie *To Please a Lady* appeared to show the character played by Barbara Stanwyck in an Indy garage. However, the controversy was defused when Indy officials insisted that Ms. Stanwyck had not entered the all-male area. The movie people had cut a hole in a fence, Ms. Stanwyck had leaned through the fence hole, and her feet had at all times been outside the garage. (In 1977, Janet Guthrie broke a major barrier to women when she became the first woman to race in the Indianapolis 500.)[221]

• In 1896, the United States Open golf tournament was held at Shinnecock Hills Golf Club. A man named John Shippen, who was part Shinnecock Indian and part West Indian, entered the tournament. However, because of his heritage, the other golfers did not want to play with Mr. Shippen and they threatened to boycott the tournament. The president of the U.S. Golf Association, Theodore Havemeyer, refused to give in to prejudice. He informed the golfers that if they boycotted the tournament, Mr. Shippen would win by default. They decided to play with Mr. Shippen.[222]

• In 1931, 17-year-old Jackie Mitchell became the first woman to sign with a men's professional baseball team when she joined the minor-league Chattanooga Lookouts. In early April of 1931, she pitched in an exhibition game against the New York Yankees and struck out Babe Ruth and Lou Gehrig, both of whom are now in the Baseball Hall of Fame. After the game, the baseball commissioner cancelled her contract because he didn't think women ought to be allowed to play professional baseball.[223]

Problem-Solving

• The spitball has been a part of baseball for a long time; even now, a professional pitcher is occasionally caught throwing a spitball. In 1912, the Pittsburgh Pirates had a spitball pitcher by the name of Marty O'Toole. The other teams knew that Mr. O'Toole was throwing spitballs, and they knew how he was doing it. His technique was to hold the ball and his glove in front of his face, then lick the ball while it was hidden by his glove. However, Philadelphia Phillies first baseman Fred Luderus figured out how to stop the pitcher from throwing spitballs. Mr. Luderus got hold of some hot liniment, and whenever he got to handle the baseball, he secretly applied some of the liniment to it. Soon, Mr. O'Toole's tongue felt like it was on fire, and he had to leave the game.[224]

• As coach of the Boston Celtics, Red Auerbach used to pull out a cigar and smoke it whenever the Celtics held a commanding lead in the final seconds of a game. This originated not so much as a way to insult other teams as a way to insult the "higher-ups" of the National Basketball Association. Mr. Auerbach once said that when the higher-ups of the NBA were picking on him, he tried to find something he could do to aggravate them. However, he didn't have any luck solving this problem until he smoked a cigar one day while coaching a game. After the game, the higher-ups sent him a note saying that smoking cigars while sitting on the bench didn't look good. Mr. Auerbach said that since reading the note, he has never been without a cigar.[225]

• United States figure skater Tara Lipinski actually started out as a roller skater. She wanted to play on a roller hockey team, but when she tried out, she was the only girl among 150 boys — some of whom had a problem skating with a girl. Fortunately, the coach, Charlie Kirchner, was very intelligent. He told 25 boys and Tara to line up with their backs to him, then told them to skate backwards to the wall. Tara reached the wall first in record time, and the boys decided that they didn't have a problem skating with a girl.[226]

• In 1913, P.E. Turnball of Lee, Massachusetts, got tired of hunters mistaking his cows for deer and shooting them. Therefore, he had several blankets made up for his cows to wear during hunting season. On the blankets appeared these words: "Don't shoot me. I am a cow." The plan worked. Mr. Turnball didn't lose any cows that year, but souvenir hunters did steal seven blankets.[227]

Rodeos

• On June 11, 1905, Zack Miller and his brothers planned to hold a Western show on their ranch located in Oklahoma's Cherokee Strip. Unfortunately, a storm headed toward the ranch and Mr. Miller worried that rain would force him and his brothers to refund the spectators' ticket money, resulting in huge losses. Suddenly, a Ponca medicine man by the name of Sits-on-a-Hill came to him and said, "Big blow. Big rain. No show." He then offered to turn the storm away from the show in return for five steers. Mr. Miller thought a moment, then he said that they had a deal. The medicine man danced and sang while beating a drum. The storm clouds neared a river, then the medicine man screamed while pointing a shell at the storm clouds. As if they had been ordered to, the storm clouds headed east, away from the Western show. The next day, after he had been paid his five steers, the medicine man told a secret to African-American rodeo star Bill Pickett. The medicine man had studied the local weather for decades, and he knew that storms almost always headed east after arriving at the river.[228]

• Gene Creed earned the title of Saddle Bronc Champion of the World in 1928, 1932, 1936, and 1938. When she was 16, her older sister was pregnant, and she was sent to her home to help out. However, while traveling to her sister's home, she noticed an advertisement in the *Denver Post* for a rodeo in Cheyenne. She had always wanted to see that part of the country, so she went to Cheyenne and competed in the rodeo, winning $300 in cash, a $75 Stetson, and a fancy belt bucket. Ms. Creed says, "I never did help my sister with the baby."[229]

Scores

• On February 19, 1982, Athens (Ohio) High School opened a 7-0 lead over Waverly High School before a Waverly player had even touched the basketball. The Waverly coach made a crucial error before the game began when he incorrectly entered the numbers of his players in the official scorebook. When the game began, the officials called five technical fouls — one for each Waverly player on the court. Athens' Steve Bruning made all five free throws, and Athens had possession of the ball and promptly scored a field goal. Score 7-0. Athens eventually won, 72-49.[230]

• The Harlem Globetrotters used to play serious basketball, playing against local teams and running up a big lead before beginning their clowning. While on tour in Woodfibre, Canada, in the early 1930s, the Globetrotters were insulted by members of the local team, who called them nasty names as they warmed up. Therefore, the Globetrotters decided to play serious basketball for the entire game. They won, 122-20.[231]

• In the 1940 NFL Championship game, the Chicago Bears defeated the Washington Redskins, 73-0. After the game, a sportswriter asked the Redskins' quarterback, Sammy Baugh, what the score might have been if a Redskin receiver had caught the football in the end zone in the first period. Mr. Baugh replied, "73 to 7."[232]

Travel

• Babe Ruth was known as much for his devotion to night life as for his devotion to hitting home runs — a fact that Ping Bodie, his roommate on New York Yankee field trips, well knew. Asked what Babe Ruth was like as a roommate, Mr. Bodie said he didn't know — he shared a room not with Babe Ruth, but with Babe Ruth's suitcase.[233]

• Wilt Chamberlain was seven feet tall, and as a Harlem Globetrotter, he traveled to many places where no one had ever seen a person that tall before. While walking down a street in Bologna, Italy, he turned around and saw 300 natives following him.[234]

Umpires

• Umpire Tom Gorman once got mad at the players in the Brooklyn Dodgers dugout because they had been riding him all game. He yelled at them to shut up, they didn't shut up, so he walked over to the dugout. At that point, he had committed himself, so he had to throw somebody out. Of course, an umpire doesn't want to hurt any team unless it is necessary, so an umpire in that situation will choose a player to throw out who isn't useful to the team — for example, a pitcher who had worked the game before. Mr. Gorman pointed in the dugout and yelled, "You're out of here, John Van Cuyk," because Mr. Van Cuyk had pitched the day before. The Brooklyn manager, Chuck Dressen, asked, "Who you want out?" Mr. Gorman repeated that he wanted Mr. Van Cuyk out, and Mr. Dressen said, "That's great, but you'll have to yell a little louder because I sent him back to the Texas League last night."[235]

• Major league baseball manager Preston Gomez sometimes was criticized by higher management for being too nice, which means they felt that he didn't argue with the umpires enough. At a time in his career when he was under fire, a close play at second base went against his club, so he came out of the dugout, told his shortstop, who was complaining, "Get back to your position. I'll handle this," then went to the umpire, Harry Wendelstedt. Out of earshot of everybody but the umpire, Mr. Gomez said, "Look, Harry, I know you got the play right and I shouldn't be out here. But they're on my *ss. They're telling me I'm not tough enough." As he talked, he performed a pantomime of a manager arguing chin to chin with an umpire. Every fan, reporter, and player thought he was mad as hell.[236]

• Late in the career of baseball umpire Bill Klem, his eyesight started to go, and of course he didn't want the baseball team managers to know that. One day, Casey Stengel and Frank Frisch, who suspected Mr. Klem's eyesight was going, cooked up a scheme. Mr. Frisch wrote out his lineup in very large letters and Mr. Stengel wrote out his lineup in very small letters. The two managers then gave their lineups to Mr. Klem, who first read Mr. Frisch's lineup out loud, then looked over Mr. Stengel's lineup and said, "That's fine." Later, Mr. Klem admitted to fellow umpire Jocko Conlan that he couldn't see Mr. Stengel's lineup: "Always have the answers, my boy. They tried to stump me. I couldn't see that lineup no more than the man in the moon. But I could still umpire."[237]

• Even as a young minor league umpire, Doug Harvey had gray hair — his hair started turning gray when he was 13 — and chewed tobacco. A pitching coach for the Philadelphia Phillies, Ray Ripplemeyer, told him, "You're a good umpire, but if you want to make it to the major leagues, you better dye your hair and get rid of that chewing tobacco." Mr. Harvey replied, "If they don't want a gray-haired, tobacco-chewing umpire, then I guess they don't want me." In a few more years, Mr. Harvey was in the major leagues as an umpire, and he went up to Mr. Ripplemeyer, spit chewing tobacco juice on his shoe, and said, "Well, I made it."[238]

• In the early days of baseball, Hugh Rorty was an umpire in New England. During a game between Lynn and Haverhill, Haverhill was leading when a fog rolled in, and the Haverhill manager requested — strongly — that the game be called on account of poor visibility, saying that he was the right fielder as well as the manager and so he knew when visibility was so bad that a game couldn't be played. Mr. Rorty simply picked up a baseball glove and went to right field, telling the Haverhill manager to hit him three flies. Mr. Rorty caught all three flies, then the game continued.[239]

• Minor league umpire Harry "Steamboat" Johnson officiated at a time when violence against umpires was not uncommon. Following a game in Nashville, some angry fans stood outside the umpires' dressing room and demanded that they come outside. Steamboat made a motion toward his hip pocket and said, "Just wait until I get this gun out and you'll leave us alone." The fans ran away, leaving Steamboat laughing because he didn't carry a gun — all he carried was a knife, which sometimes came in handy in such situations.[240]

• In the Pacific Coast League, San Diego catcher Del Ballinger protested a called strike by umpire Gordon Ford by pulling out a pistol, pointing it to the umpire's chest, and firing three times. Mr. Ford's face went white until he realized that the pistol was a harmless toy cap pistol. Of course, Mr. Ford threw Mr. Ballinger out of the game, but that didn't mean he was without a sense of humor. When the next player came up to bat, Mr. Ford frisked him to see if he was carrying any hidden weapons.[241]

• Umpire Clarence "Pants" Rowland once called out Babe Ruth on a close play at third base one day, but he also praised him, helping him up, brushing off his uniform, and saying, "Great slide, Babe, but he just had you." The Yankee players wondered why Babe didn't argue the call, but Babe explained, "What could I do? I thought I was safe, but the guy was dusting my clothes off and telling me what a great slide I made. What could I say to him?"[242]

• Umpire Beans Reardon once made a mistake. Richie Ashburn slid into second base and Billy Cox attempted to tag him. Beans yelled "Safe," but at the same time he flung his arm in the "Out" gesture. Mr. Ashburn asked, "What the hell does that mean?" Mr. Reardon replied, "Richie, you know you're safe. Billy, you know he's safe. But 30,000 fans see my arm. Richie, you're out."[243]

• In 1939, Bob Dillinger was batting in the Western League when he thought the umpire made a bad call by calling a ball his second strike. Mr. Dillinger took off his glasses, then handed them to the umpire, who shocked him by putting them on and yelling "Play ball!" The next pitch came, and the umpire yelled "Strike three," then handed the glasses back to Mr. Dillinger.[244]

• Greg "the Bull" Luzinski was a big man and a major hitter in the major leagues. Umpire Eric Gregg once called a strike on him, and when the next pitch went across the plate at roughly the same spot, he called, "That's two." The Bull raised the bat above his head and asked, "Two what?" Mr. Gregg looked at the baseball bat and the Bull's massive build and replied, "Too high."[245]

• Charlie Grimm, manager of the Chicago Cubs, once got angry with umpire Charlie Moran — so did several of his players. As his players stormed out to argue the call with umpire Moran, Mr. Grimm told them, "The first person to lay a finger on this blind old man will be fined 50 bucks."[246]

Uniforms

• When Elfi Schlegel was competing in gymnastics at the University of Florida, football running back Neal Anderson, who played for the Chicago Bears in the 1980s, was a frequent visitor to the gymnastics practices. He had a good reason for working on his tumbling: After scoring a touchdown, he would perform a back flip in the end zone while still dressed in his football uniform.[247]

• Football player O.J. Simpson has a big head — literally. When he started playing for the Buffalo Bills, he couldn't practice hard because no helmet would fit him. One of his old college helmets had to be brought in from his alma mater — the University of Southern California.[248]

War

• During World War II, many major league baseball players such as Joe DiMaggio went into the Armed Forces, and people weren't sure that major league baseball could continue during the war. To ensure inexpensive sports entertainment during the war, Philip K. Wrigley (owner of the Chicago Cubs and manufacturer of the chewing gum) started the All American Girls Professional Baseball League. When the teams lined up on the baseball field for the singing of the national anthem before a game, they always lined up in a V formation because "V is for Victory."[249]

• Soviet gymnast Olga Korbut won several medals at the 1972 Olympic Games in Munich and won the hearts of fans worldwide. Her father, Valentin, was only 15 when Nazi soldiers came into the village he lived in near Kalinkovich in Belorussia. Despite his age, he participated in some of the ambushes the Soviets laid against the Nazis, and he helped set up mines that destroyed Nazi trains and motor vehicles.[250]

Appendix A: Bibliography

Aaseng, Nate. *Great Winter Olympic Moments*. Minneapolis, MN: Lerner Publications Company, 1990.

Adelson, Bruce. *Grand Slam Trivia*. Minneapolis, MN: Lerner Publications Company, 1999.

Barich, Bill. *The Sporting Life: Horses, Boxers, Rivers, and a Soviet Ballclub*. New York: The Lyons Press, 1999.

Belle, Albert. *Don't Call Me Joey: The Wit and Wisdom of Albert Belle*. Toronto, Canada: ECW Press, 1998.

Berke, Art. *Babe Ruth*. New York: Franklin Watts, 1988.

Berra, Yogi. *"I Really Didn't Say Everything I Said."* New York: Workman Publishing Company, Inc., 1998.

Bezic, Sandra. *The Passion to Skate: An Intimate View of Figure Skating*. With David Hayes. Atlanta, GA: Turner Publishing, Inc., 1996.

Bontemps, Arna. *Famous Negro Athletes*. New York: Dodd, Mead, and Company, 1964.

Brennan, Christine. *Inside Edge: A Revealing Journey into the Secret World of Figure Skating*. New York: Scribner, 1996.

Brown, Cordell. *I am What I am by the Grace of God*. Warsaw, OH: Echoing Hills Village Foundation, 1996.

Brown, Joe E. *Laughter is a Wonderful Thing*. As told to Ralph Hancock. New York: A.S. Barnes and Co., 1956.

Buck, Ray. *Tiffany Chin: A Dream on Ice*. Chicago, IL: Children's Press, 1986.

Burchard, S.H. *Tracy Austin*. New York: Harcourt Brace Jovanovich, Publishers, 1982.

Cantwell, Lois, and Pohla Smith. *Women Winners: Then and Now*. New York: Sports Illustrated for Kids, 2000.

Châtaigneau, Gérard, and Steve Milton. *Figure Skating Now: Olympic and World Stars*. Willowdale, Ontario, Canada: Firefly Books, 2001.

Chisholm, Rod. *The Athletic Banquet Speaker*. The Author: Des Moines, IA, 1957.

Conlan, Jocko and Robert W. Creamer. *Jocko*. Lincoln, NE: University of Nebraska Press, 1997.

Conner, Bart. *Winning the Gold*. With Coach Paul Ziert. New York: Warner Books, Inc., 1985.

Coombs, Karen Mueller. *Jackie Robinson: Baseball's Civil Rights Legend*. Springfield, NJ: Enslow Publications, Inc., 1997.

Cranston, Toller. *Zero Tollerance*. With Martha Lowder Kimball. Toronto, Canada: McClelland and Stewart, Inc., 1997.

Crum, Jimmy, and Carole Gerber. *How About That! Jimmy Crum: Fifty Years of Cliffhangers and Barn-Burners*. Columbus, OH: Fine Line Graphics, 1993.

Davis, Rebecca. *The Story of the Washington Mystics*. Mankato, MN: Creative Education, 2000.

Donovan, Pete. *Carol Johnston: The One-Armed Gymnast*. Chicago, IL: Children's Press, 1982.

Durrett, Deanne. *Dominique Moceanu*. San Diego, CA: Lucent Books, 1999.

Feather, Leonard, and Jack Tracy. *Laughter from the Hip: The Lighter Side of Jazz*. New York: Da Capo Press, Inc., 1979.

Fleming, Peggy. *The Long Program*. With Peter Kaminsky. New York: Pocket Books, 1999.

Galt, Margot Fortunato. *Up to the Plate: The All American Girls Professional Baseball League*. Minneapolis, MN: Lerner Publications Company, 1995.

Garagiola, Joe. *Baseball is a Funny Game*. New York: Bantam Books, 1960.

Garagiola, Joe. *It's Anybody's Ballgame*. New York: Jove Books, 1988.

Goldstein, Margaret J. *Jennifer Capriati: Tennis Sensation*. Minneapolis, MN: Lerner Publications Company, 1993.

Golubev, Vladimir. *Soviet Gymnastics Stars*. Translated by Yuri Nemetsky. Photographs by Vladimir Safronov. Moscow: Progress Publishers, 1979.

Goodman, Jack, and Albert Rice. *I Wish I'd Said That!* New York: Simon and Schuster, 1935.

Gordeeva, Ekaterina. *My Sergei: A Love Story*. With E.M. Swift. New York: Warner Books, Inc., 1996.

Gorman, Tom, and Jerome Holtzman. *Three and Two!* New York: Charles Scribner's Sons, 1979.

Gregg, Eric, and Marty Appel. *Working the Plate: The Eric Gregg Story*. New York: William Morrow and Company, Inc., 1990.

Gutman, Bill. *Barry Sanders: Football's Rushing Champ*. Brookfield, CT: The Millbrook Press, 1993.

Gutman, Bill. *The Harlem Globetrotters: Basketball's Funniest Team*. Champaign, IL: Garrard Publishing Company, 1977.

Gutman, Dan. *Gymnastics: The Trials, the Triumphs, the Truth*. New York: Puffin Books, 1996.

Haney, Lynn. *The Lady is a Jock*. New York: Dodd, Mead, and Company, 1973.

Haney, Lynn. *Ride 'em, Cowgirl!* New York: G.P. Putnam's Sons, 1975.

Hay, Peter. *Canned Laughter*. New York: Oxford University Press, 1992.

Hyams, Joe. *Zen in the Martial Arts*. New York: Bantam Books, 1979.

Jacobs, Linda. *Evonne Goolagong: Smiles and Smashes*. St. Paul, MN: EMI Corporation, 1975.

Jacobs, Linda. *Janet Lynn: Sunshine on Ice*. St. Paul, MN: EMC Corporation, 1974.

Jessel, George. *This Way, Miss*. New York: Henry Holt and Company, 1955.

Johnson, Harry "Steamboat." *Standing the Gaff: The Life and Hard Times of a Minor League Umpire*. Introduction to the Bison Book edition by Larry R. Gerlach. Lincoln, NE: University of Nebraska Press, 1994.

Jones, Betty Millsaps. *Wonder Women of Sports*. New York: Random House, 1981.

Karolyi, Bela, and Nancy Ann Richardson. *Feel No Fear: The Power, Passion, and Politics of a Life in Gymnastics*. New York: Hyperion, 1994.

Kilduff, Lee. *Sports Heroines*. Chicago, IL: Kidsbooks, Inc., 1993.

Kleinbaum, Nancy H. *The Magnificent Seven: The Authorized Story of American Gold*. New York: Bantam Books, 1996.

Knapp, Ron. *Sports Great Bo Jackson*. Hillside, NJ: Enslow Publications, Inc., 1990.

Knudson, R.R. *Babe Didrikson: Athlete of the Century*. New York: Puffin Books, 1985.

Knudson, R.R. *Martina Navratilova: Tennis Power*. New York: Viking Kestrel, 1986.

Koral, April. *Florence Griffith Joyner: Track and Field Star*. New York: Franklin Watts, 1992.

Kwan, Michelle and Laura James. *Michelle Kwan: Heart of a Champion*. New York: Scholastic, Inc., 1997.

Lessa, Christina. *Gymnastics Balancing Acts*. New York: Universe Publishing, 1997.

Lessa, Christina. *Women Who Win: Stories of Triumph in Sport and in Life*. New York: Universe Publishing, 1998.

Linkletter, Art. *I Wish I'd Said That! My Favorite Ad-Libs of All Time*. Garden City, New York: Doubleday & Co., Inc., 1968.

Lipinski, Tara. *Totally Tara: An Olympic Journey*. Original photography by Simon Bruty, with text by Mark Zeigler. New York: Universe, 1998.

Lipinski, Tara, and Emily Costello. *Tara Lipinski: Triumph on Ice*. New York: Bantam Books, 1997.

Long, Barbara. *Jim Thorpe: Legendary Athlete*. Springfield, NJ: Enslow Publications, Inc., 1997.

Lovitt, Chip. *American Gymnasts: Gold Medal Dreams*. New York: Pocket Books, 2000.

Mackenzie, Richard. *A Wee Nip at the 19th Hole: A History of the St. Andrews Caddie*. Chelsea, MI: Sleeping Bear Press, 1997.

Macnow, Glen. *Sports Great Charles Barkley*. Hillside, NJ: Enslow Publications, Inc., 1992.

Maverick, Jr., Maury. *Texas Iconoclast*. Edited by Allan O. Kownslar. Fort Worth, TX: Texas Christian University Press, 1997.

May, Julian. *Billie Jean King: Tennis Champion*. Mankato, MN: Crestwood House, Inc., 1974.

Meyer, Miriam Weiss, Project Editor. *Top Picks: People*. Pleasantville, NY: Reader's Digest Educational Division, 1977.

Miller, Claudia. *Shannon Miller: My Child, My Hero*. Norman, OK: University of Oklahoma Press, 1999.

Miller, Shannon. *Winning Every Day: Gold Medal Advice for a Happy, Healthy Life!* New York: Bantam Books, 1998.

Milton, Steve. *Skate Talk: Figure Skating in the Words of the Stars*. Buffalo, NY: Firefly Books, Inc., 1997.

Moceanu, Dominique. *Dominique Moceanu, An American Champion: An Autobiography*. As told to Steve Woodward. New York: Bantam Doubleday Dell Publishing Group, Inc., 1996.

Mockridge, Norton. *A Funny Thing Happened ....* Greenwich, CT: Fawcett Publications, Inc., 1966.

Mullen, Tom. *Seriously, Life is a Laughing Matter*. Waco, TX: Word Books, 1978.

Norkin, Sam. *Drawings, Stories: Theater, Opera, Ballet, Movies*. Portsmouth, NH: Heinemann, 1994.

Olney, Ross R. *Lyn St. James: Driven to Be First*. Minneapolis, MN: Lerner Publications Company, 1997.

Pellowski, Michael J. *Baseball's Funniest People*. New York: Sterling Publishing Co., 1997.

Peszek, Luan. *The Gymnastics Almanac*. Chicago, IL: Lowell House, 1998.

Pietrusza, David. *The Boston Celtics Basketball Team*. Springfield, NJ: Enslow Publications, Inc., 1998.

Poynter, Margaret. *Top 10 American Women's Figure Skaters*. Springfield, NJ: Enslow Publications, Inc., 1998.

Quiner, Krista. *Dominique Moceanu: A Gymnastics Sensation*. East Hanover, NJ: The Bradford Book Company, 1997.

Raber, Thomas R. *Michael Jordan: Basketball Skywalker*. Minneapolis, MN: Lerner Publications Company, 1997.

Retton, Mary Lou, and Bela Karolyi. *Mary Lou: Creating an Olympic Champion*. With John Powers. New York: McGraw-Hill Book Company, 1986.

Richie, Donald. *Zen Inklings*. New York: John Weatherhill, Inc., 1982.

Rogers, Dave. *The Avengers*. London: Independent Television Books, Ltd., 1983.

Rosenthal, Bert. *Lynette Woodard: The First Female Globetrotter*. Chicago, IL: Children's Press, 1986.

Rosten, Leo. *People I Have Loved, Known or Admired*. New York: McGraw-Hill Book Company, 1970.

Russell, Fred, teller. *Funny Thing About Sports*. Nashville, TN: The McQuiddy Press, 1948.

Russell, Fred. *I'll Try Anything Twice*. Nashville, TN: The McQuiddy Press, 1945.

Rutledge, Rachel. *The Best of the Best in Gymnastics*. Brookfield, CT: The Millbrook Press, 1999.

Samra, Cal and Rose, editors. *More Holy Hilarity*. Colorado Springs, CO: WaterBrook Press, 1999.

Sanford, William R., and Carl R. Green. *Bill Pickett: African-American Rodeo Star*. Springfield, NJ: Enslow Publications, Inc., 1997.

Sanford, William R., and Carl R. Green. *Dorothy Hamill*. New York: Crestwood House, 1993.

Savage, Jeff. *Tiger Woods: King of the Course*. Minneapolis, MN: Lerner Publications Company, 1998.

Schafer, Kermit. *All Time Great Bloopers*. New York: Avenel Books, 1973.

Schlegel, Elfi, and Claire Ross Dunn. *The Gymnastics Book: The Young Performer's Guide to Gymnastics*. Buffalo, NY: Firefly Books, Inc., 2001.

Schleichert, Elizabeth. *Dave Bing: Basketball Great with a Heart*. Springfield, NJ: Enslow Publications, Inc., 1995.

Schulman, Arlene. *Muhammad Ali: Champion*. Minneapolis, MN: Lerner Publications Company, 1996.

Silverstein, Herma. *Mary Lou Retton and the New Gymnasts*. New York: Franklin Watts, 1985.

Skipper, John C. *Umpires: Classic Baseball Stories from the Men Who Made the Calls*. Jefferson, NC, and London: McFarland and Company, Inc., Publishers, 1997.

Smith, Beverley. *Figure Skating: A Celebration*. Toronto, Ontario, Canada: McClelland & Stewart, Inc., 1994.

Smith, Beverley. *Talking Figure Skating*. Toronto, Ontario, Canada: McClelland & Stewart Inc., 1997.

Smith, Ira L. and H. Allen Smith. *Low and Inside*. Garden City, New York: Doubleday and Company, Inc., 1949.

Smith, Ira L., and H. Allen Smith. *Three Men on Third*. New York: Doubleday & Co., Inc., 1951.

Snead, Sam. *The Game I Love: Wisdom, Insight, and Instruction from Golf's Greatest Player*. With Fran Pirozzolo. New York: Ballantine Books, 1997.

Sobol, Donald J. *Encyclopedia Brown's Book of the Wacky Outdoors*. New York: William Morrow and Company, Inc., 1987.

Sobol, Donald J. *Encyclopedia Brown's Book of Wacky Sports*. New York: William Morrow and Company, 1984.

Straus, Hal, editor. *Gymnastics Guide*. Mountain View, CA: World Publications, 1978.

Streissguth, Tom. *Jesse Owens*. Minneapolis, MN: Lerner Publications Company, 1999.

Strug, Kerri. *Landing on My Feet: A Diary of Dreams*. With John P. Lopez. Kansas City, MO: Andrews McMeel Publishing, 1997.

Sullivan, George. *Any Number Can Play*. New York: Thomas Y. Crowell, 1990.

Suponev, Michael. *Olga Korbut: A Biographical Portrait*. Garden City, NY: Doubleday and Company, Inc., 1975.

Thomas, Kurt, and Kent Hannon. *Kurt Thomas on Gymnastics*. New York: Simon and Schuster, 1980.

Thompson, Joe. *Growing Up with "Shoeless Joe."* Greenville, SC: Burgess International, 1997.

Torres, John A. *Greg Maddux: Ace!* Minneapolis, MN: Lerner Publications Company, 1997.

Torvill, Jayne, and Christopher Dean. *Torvill and Dean: The Autobiography of Ice Dancing's Greatest Stars*. With John Man. Secaucus, NJ: Carol Publishing Group, 1996.

Tully, Jim. *A Dozen and One*. Hollywood, CA: Murray & Gee, Inc., Publishers, 1943.

Udall, Morris K. *Too Funny to be President*. With Bob Neuman and Randy Udall. New York: Henry Holt and Company, 1988.

Uecker, Bob, and Mickey Herskowitz. *Catcher in the Wry*. New York: G.P. Putnam's Sons, 1982.

Uschan, Michael V. *Male Olympic Champions*. San Diego, CA: Lucent Books, 2000.

Van Steenwyk, Elizabeth. *Rodeo*. New York: Harvey House, Publishers, 1978.

Wade, Don. *"And Then Arnie Told Chi Chi ...."* Chicago, IL: Contemporary Books, 1993.

Ward, Gene, and Dick Hyman, collectors. *Football Wit and Humor*. New York: Grosset & Dunlap, Publishers, 1970.

Weatherby, W.J. *Jackie Gleason: An Intimate Portrait*. New York: Berkley Books, 1992.

Wilner, Barry. *Michelle Kwan: Star Figure Skater*. Berkeley Heights, NJ: Enslow Publications, Inc., 2001.

Wood, Rob, editor. *It's All in the Game: Funny Happenings for Those Who Love Sports*. Kansas City, MO: Hallmark Cards, Inc., 1976.

Wright, David K. *Arthur Ashe: Breaking the Color Barrier in Tennis*. Springfield, NJ: Enslow Publications, Inc., 1996.

Zolotow, Maurice. *No People Like Show People*. New York: Random House, 1951.

Appendix B: About the Author

It was a dark and stormy night. Suddenly a cry rang out, and on a hot summer night in 1954, Josephine, wife of Carl Bruce, gave birth to a boy — me. Unfortunately, this young married couple allowed Reuben Saturday, Josephine's brother, to name their first-born. Reuben, aka "The Joker," decided that Bruce was a nice name, so he decided to name me Bruce Bruce. I have gone by my middle name — David — ever since.

Being named Bruce David Bruce hasn't been all bad. Bank tellers remember me very quickly, so I don't often have to show an ID. It can be fun in charades, also. When I was a counselor as a teenager at Camp Echoing Hills in Warsaw, Ohio, a fellow counselor gave the signs for "sounds like" and "two words," then she pointed to a bruise on her leg twice. Bruise Bruise? Oh yeah, Bruce Bruce is the answer!

Uncle Reuben, by the way, is the guy who gave me a haircut when I was in kindergarten. He cut my hair short and shaved a small bald spot on the back of my head. My mother wouldn't let me go to school until the bald spot grew out again.

Of all my brothers and sisters (six in all), I am the only transplant to Athens, Ohio. I was born in Newark, Ohio, and have lived all around Southeastern Ohio. However, I moved to Athens to go to Ohio University and have never left.

At OU, I never could make up my mind whether to major in English or Philosophy, so I got a Bachelor's with a double major in both areas in 1980, then I added a master's degree in English in 1984 and a master's degree in Philosophy in 1985. Currently, and for a long time to come, I publish a weekly humorous column titled "Wise Up!" for *The Athens NEWS* and I am a retired English instructor at OU.

Appendix C: Some Books by David Bruce

Anecdote Collections

250 Anecdotes About Opera

250 Anecdotes About Religion

250 Anecdotes About Religion: Volume 2

250 Music Anecdotes

Be a Work of Art: 250 Anecdotes and Stories

The Coolest People in Art: 250 Anecdotes

The Coolest People in the Arts: 250 Anecdotes

The Coolest People in Books: 250 Anecdotes

The Coolest People in Comedy: 250 Anecdotes

Create, Then Take a Break: 250 Anecdotes

Don't Fear the Reaper: 250 Anecdotes

The Funniest People in Art: 250 Anecdotes

The Funniest People in Books: 250 Anecdotes

The Funniest People in Books, Volume 2: 250 Anecdotes

The Funniest People in Books, Volume 3: 250 Anecdotes

The Funniest People in Comedy: 250 Anecdotes

The Funniest People in Dance: 250 Anecdotes

The Funniest People in Families: 250 Anecdotes

The Funniest People in Families, Volume 2: 250 Anecdotes

The Funniest People in Families, Volume 3: 250 Anecdotes

The Funniest People in Families, Volume 4: 250 Anecdotes

The Funniest People in Families, Volume 5: 250 Anecdotes

The Funniest People in Families, Volume 6: 250 Anecdotes

The Funniest People in Movies: 250 Anecdotes

The Funniest People in Music: 250 Anecdotes

The Funniest People in Music, Volume 2: 250 Anecdotes

The Funniest People in Music, Volume 3: 250 Anecdotes

The Funniest People in Neighborhoods: 250 Anecdotes

The Funniest People in Relationships: 250 Anecdotes

The Funniest People in Sports: 250 Anecdotes

The Funniest People in Sports, Volume 2: 250 Anecdotes

The Funniest People in Television and Radio: 250 Anecdotes

The Funniest People in Theater: 250 Anecdotes

The Funniest People Who Live Life: 250 Anecdotes

The Funniest People Who Live Life, Volume 2: 250 Anecdotes

The Kindest People Who Do Good Deeds, Volume 1: 250 Anecdotes

The Kindest People Who Do Good Deeds, Volume 2: 250 Anecdotes

Maximum Cool: 250 Anecdotes

The Most Interesting People in Movies: 250 Anecdotes

The Most Interesting People in Politics and History: 250 Anecdotes

The Most Interesting People in Politics and History, Volume 2: 250 Anecdotes

The Most Interesting People in Politics and History, Volume 3: 250 Anecdotes

The Most Interesting People in Religion: 250 Anecdotes

The Most Interesting People in Sports: 250 Anecdotes

The Most Interesting People Who Live Life: 250 Anecdotes

The Most Interesting People Who Live Life, Volume 2: 250 Anecdotes

Reality is Fabulous: 250 Anecdotes and Stories

Resist Psychic Death: 250 Anecdotes

Seize the Day: 250 Anecdotes and Stories

[1] Source: Betty Millsaps Jones, *Wonder Women of Sports*, pp. 52-54.

[2] Source: Julian May, *Billie Jean King: Tennis Champion*, pp. 36-37.

[3] Source: Donald J. Sobol, *Encyclopedia Brown's Book of the Wacky Outdoors*, p. 49.

[4] Source: David K. Wright, *Arthur Ashe: Breaking the Color Barrier in Tennis*, p. 61.

[5] Source: Ron Knapp, *Sports Great Bo Jackson*, p. 28.

[6] Source: Richard Mackenzie, *A Wee Nip at the 19th Hole*, pp. 98-99.

[7] Source: Toller Cranston, *Zero Tollerance*, pp. 205-208.

[8] Source: William R. Sanford and Carl R. Green, *Bill Pickett: African-American Rodeo Star*, pp. 10-12, 28, 38.

[9] Source: Lynn Haney, *The Lady is a Jock*, p. 173.

[10] Source: Toller Cranston, *Zero Tollerance*, pp. 197-201.

[11] Source: Vladimir Golubev, *Soviet Gymnastics Stars*, p. 190.

[12] Source: Jimmy Crum and Carole Gerber, *How About That!*, pp. 35-36.

[13] Source: Steve Milton, *Skate Talk: Figure Skating in the Words of the Stars*, p. 25.

[14] Source: Claudia Miller, *Shannon Miller: My Child, My Hero*, p. 42.

[15] Source: Deanne Durrett, *Dominique Moceanu*, p. 42.

[16] Source: Joe Thompson, *Growing Up with "Shoeless Joe,"* pp. 121-122.

[17] Source: A channel 4 NBC newscast in Columbus, Ohio.

[18] Source: Ekaterina Gordeeva, *My Sergei*, p. 180.

[19] Source: Tom Mullen, *Seriously, Life is a Laughing Matter*, pp. 57-58.

[20] Source: Tara Lipinski and Emily Costello, *Tara Lipinski: Triumph on Ice*, pp. 13-16.

[21] Source: Lee Kilduff, *Sports Heroines*, pp. 38-40.

[22] Source: Eric Gregg and Marty Appel, *Working the Plate*, p. 35.

[23] Source: Arlene Schulman, *Muhammad Ali: Champion*, pp. 17-18, 20.

[24] Source: Bert Rosenthal, *Lynette Woodard: The First Female Globetrotter*, pp. 10, 12, 15, 25, 46.

[25] Source: Dominique Moceanu, *Dominique Moceanu, An American Champion*, p. 7.

[26] Source: The NBC presentation of the 2000 Pontiac Women's Gymnastics Team Championships.

[27] Source: Christina Lessa, *Gymnastics Balancing Acts*, p. 8.

[28] Source: Bart Conner, *Winning the Gold*, p. 14.

[29] Source: Claudia Miller, *Shannon Miller: My Child, My Hero*, p. 20.

[30] Source: Margaret J. Goldstein, *Jennifer Capriati: Tennis Sensation*, pp. 14-15.

[31] Source: Mary Lou Retton and Bela Karolyi, *Mary Lou: Creating an Olympic Champion*, p. 3.

[32] Source: Gérard Châtaigneau and Steve Milton, *Figure Skating Now: Olympic and World Stars*, p. 57.

[33] Source: Chip Lovitt, *American Gymnasts: Gold Medal Dreams*, p. 63.

[34] Source: John A. Torres, *Greg Maddux: Ace!*, p. 22.

[35] Source: Margaret J. Goldstein, *Jennifer Capriati: Tennis Sensation*, p. 31.

[36] Source: Elfi Schlegel and Claire Ross Dunn, *The Gymnastics Book*, p. 116.

[37] Source: Luan Peszek, *The Gymnastics Almanac*, p. 97.

[38] Source: Linda Jacobs, *Evonne Goolagong: Smiles and Smashes*, pp. 17-18.

[39] Source: Lynn Haney, *Ride 'em, Cowgirl!*, p. 55.

[40] Source: Sam Snead, *The Game I Love*, p. 214.

[41] Source: April Koral, *Florence Griffith Joyner: Track and Field Star*, pp. 9, 22, 38, 40, 42, 45.

[42] Source: Michelle Kwan and Laura James, *Michelle Kwan*, pp. 44-45.

[43] Source: Sandra Bezic, *The Passion to Skate*, p. 85.

[44] Source: Bruce Adelson, *Grand Slam Trivia*, pp. 12-13.

[45] Source: Yogi Berra, *"I Really Didn't Say Everything I Said,"* p. 43.

[46] Source: Beverley Smith, *Talking Figure Skating*, p. 118.

[47] Source: Michelle Kwan and Laura James, *Michelle Kwan*, p. 42.

[48] Source: Fred Russell, *I'll Try Anything Twice*, p. 79.

[49] Source: Rod Chisholm, *The Athletic Banquet Speaker*, p. 9.

[50] Source: Joe E. Brown, *Laughter is a Wonderful Thing*, p. 91.

[51] Source: Leo Rosten, *People I Have Loved, Known or Admired*, p. 61.

[52] Source: W.J. Weatherby, *Jackie Gleason: An Intimate Portrait*, p. 40.

[53] Source: Job Bob Briggs, "Joe Bob's America" column. 6 April 1990 <http://www.joebobbriggs.com/jbamerica/1990/jba900406.html>.

[54] Source: Nancy H. Kleinbaum, *The Magnificent Seven*, pp. 86, 91.

[55] Source: Don Wade, *"And Then Arnie Told Chi Chi...,"* p. 116.

[56] Source: Tara Lipinski, *Totally Tara: An Olympic Journey*, p. 15.

[57] Source: Krista Quiner, *Dominique Moceanu: A Gymnastics Sensation*, p. 69.

[58] Source: Lois Cantwell and Pohla Smith, *Women Winners: Then and Now*, pp. 52, 55.

[59] Source: Dan Gutman, *Gymnastics: The Trials, the Triumphs, the Truth*, pp. 162-163.

[60] Source: Linda Jacobs, *Janet Lynn: Sunshine on Ice*, pp. 33-34.

[61] Source: Rachel Rutledge, *The Best of the Best in Gymnastics*, pp. 27-28.

[62] Source: Leonard Feather and Jack Tracy, *Laughter from the Hip: The Lighter Side of Jazz*, pp. 8-9.

[63] Source: Gérard Châtaigneau and Steve Milton, *Figure Skating Now: Olympic and World Stars*, p. 7.

[64] Source: Fred Russell, *I'll Try Anything Twice*, p. 22.

[65] Source: Bill Gutman, *The Harlem Globetrotters*, p. 19.

[66] Source: R.R. Knudson, *Babe Didrikson: Athlete of the Century*, pp. 54, 56.

[67] Source: John C. Skipper, *Umpires*, p. 16.

[68] Source: Tom Gorman and Jerome Holtzman, *Three and Two!*, p. 120.

[69] Source: Glen Macnow, *Sports Great Charles Barkley*, pp. 11-12, 16, 18.

[70] Source: Pete Donovan, *Carol Johnston: The One-Armed Gymnast*, pp. 27-28.

[71] Source: Rebecca Davis, *The Story of the Washington Mystics*, p. 17.

[72] Source: Chip Lovitt, *American Gymnasts: Gold Medal Dreams*, p. 64.

[73] Source: Arlene Schulman, *Muhammad Ali: Champion*, p. 21.

[74] Source: Joe Hyams, *Zen in the Martial Arts*, pp. 69-70.

[75] Source: Margaret Poynter, *Top 10 American Women's Figure Skaters*, pp. 38, 40.

[76] Source: Shannon Miller, *Winning Every Day*, p. 103.

[77] Source: Lois Cantwell and Pohla Smith, *Women Winners: Then and Now*, p. 12.

[78] Source: Cordell Brown, *I am What I am by the Grace of God*, pp. 25-26.

[79] Source: Arna Bontemps, *Famous Negro Athletes*, p. 109.

[80] Source: A column by Dan Lynch of the Albany (NY) *Times Union*.

[81] Source: Norton Mockridge, *A Funny Thing Happened ...*, pp. 27-28.

[82] Source: Jayne Torvill and Christopher Dean, *Torvill and Dean*, pp. 84-85.

[83] Source: Ron Knapp, *Sports Great Bo Jackson*, pp. 28-29.

[84] Source: Kurt Thomas and Kent Hannon, *Kurt Thomas on Gymnastics*, p. 73.

[85] Source: Rod Chisholm, *The Athletic Banquet Speaker*, p. 18.

[86] Source: Shannon Miller, *Winning Every Day*, p. 119.

[87] Source: Thomas R. Raber, *Michael Jordan: Basketball Skywalker*, p. 24.

[88] Source: Linda Jacobs, *Janet Lynn: Sunshine on Ice*, pp. 22, 29.

[89] Source: Hal Straus, editor, *Gymnastics Guide*, p. 351.

[90] Source: Harry "Steamboat" Johnson, *Standing the Gaff*, p. 87.

[91] Source: Vladimir Golubev, *Soviet Gymnastics Stars*, p. 62.

[92] Source: Dan Gutman, *Gymnastics: The Trials, the Triumphs, the Truth*, pp. 50-51.

[93] Source: Luan Peszek, *The Gymnastics Almanac*, p. 99.

[94] Source: Michael Suponev, *Olga Korbut*, pp. 49-50.

[95] Source: Maurice Zolotow, *No People Like Show People*, pp. 35-36.

[96] Source: Jack Goodman and Albert Rice, *I Wish I'd Said That!*, p. 65.

[97] Source: Christina Lessa, *Women Who Win*, p. 47.

[98] Source: Beverley Smith, *Figure Skating: A Celebration*, p. 83.

[99] Source: Lynn Haney, *The Lady is a Jock*, pp. 61, 63, 125-126.

[100] Source: Dave Rogers, *The Avengers*, p. 29.

[101] Source: Kermit Schafer, *All Time Great Bloopers*, p. 13.

[102] Source: Donald Richie, *Zen Inklings*, pp. 106-107.

[103] Source: Karen Mueller Coombs, *Jackie Robinson: Baseball's Civil Rights Legend*, p. 20.

[104] Source: Bill Barich, *The Sporting Life: Horses, Boxers, Rivers, and a Soviet Ballclub*, p. 116.

[105] Source: David Pietrusza, *The Boston Celtics Basketball Team*, pp. 25, 27.

[106] Source: Beverley Smith, *Figure Skating: A Celebration*, pp. 20-21.

[107] Source: Elizabeth Van Steenwyk, *Rodeo*, pp. 9-10.

[108] Source: Glen Macnow, *Sports Great Charles Barkley*, pp. 20-21, 35.

[109] Source: Kerri Strug, *Landing on My Feet*, p. 51.

[110] Source: Krista Quiner, *Dominique Moceanu: A Gymnastics Sensation*, pp. 22-23.

[111] Source: Christine Brennan, *Inside Edge*, p. 206.

[112] Source: S.H. Burchard, *Tracy Austin*, pp. 28, 36, 63.

[113] Source: Peter Hay, *Canned Laughter*, 209-210.

[114] Source: Ekaterina Gordeeva, *My Sergei*, p. 84.

[115] Source: R.R. Knudson, *Martina Navratilova: Tennis Power*, p. 23.

[116] Source: Michael V. Uschan, *Male Olympic Champions*, p. 53.

[117] Source: R.R. Knudson, *Martina Navratilova: Tennis Power*, pp. 38, 40.

[118] Source: Jim Tully, *A Dozen and One*, pp. 173-174.

[119] Source: Miriam Weiss Meyer, project editor, *Top Picks: People*, p. 50.

[120] Source: Sam Snead, *The Game I Love*, p. 80.

[121] Source: Albert Belle, *Don't Call Me Joey*, p. 17, 39.

[122] Source: Margot Fortunato Galt, *Up to the Plate: The All American Girls Professional Baseball League*, p. 69.

[123] Source: Elizabeth Schleichert, *Dave Bing: Basketball Great with a Heart*, pp. 66, 68.

[124] Source: Nate Aaseng, *Great Winter Olympic Moments*, p. 36.

[125] Source: Bill Gutman, *Barry Sanders: Football's Rushing Champ*, pp. 14-15.

[126] Source: Linda Jacobs, *Evonne Goolagong: Smiles and Smashes*, pp. 7, 18.

[127] Source: Herma Silverstein, *Mary Lou Retton and the New Gymnasts*, pp. 48, 51.

[128] Source: Julian May, *Billie Jean King: Tennis Champion*, p. 20.

[129] Source: Bill Gutman, *Barry Sanders: Football's Rushing Champ*, p. 13.

[130] Source: Nate Aaseng, *Great Winter Olympic Moments*, p. 25.

[131] Source: Thomas R. Raber, *Michael Jordan: Basketball Skywalker*, p. 26.

[132] Source: Ira L. Smith and H. Allen Smith, *Three Men on Third*, p. 116.

[133] Source: Joe Garagiola, *Baseball is a Funny Game*, p. 43.

[134] Source: Leo Rosten, *People I Have Loved, Known or Admired*, p. 254.

[135] Source: Art Berke, *Babe Ruth*, p. 60.

[136] Source: Yogi Berra, *"I Really Didn't Say Everything I Said,"* p. 13.

[137] Source: Joe Thompson, *Growing Up with "Shoeless Joe,"* p. 121.

[138] Source: Bob Uecker and Mickey Herskowitz, *Catcher in the Wry*, pp. 182-183.

[139] Source: Tom Streissguth, *Jesse Owens*, p. 70.

[140] Source: Rob Wood, editor, *It's All in the Game: Funny Happenings for Those Who Love Sports*, p. 11.

[141] Source: Kurt Thomas and Kent Hannon, *Kurt Thomas on Gymnastics*, p. 188.

[142] Source: Maury Maverick, Jr., *Texas Iconoclast*, pp. 270-271.

[143] Source: Elizabeth Van Steenwyk, *Rodeo*, p. 76.

[144] Source: Bela Karolyi and Nancy Ann Richardson, *Feel No Fear*, p. 192.

[145] Source: Mary Lou Retton and Bela Karolyi, *Mary Lou: Creating an Olympic Champion*, p. 62.

[146] Source: Maury Maverick, Jr., *Texas Iconoclast*, p. 5.

[147] Source: Deanne Durrett, *Dominique Moceanu*, p. 15.

[148] Source: Jim Tully, *A Dozen and One*, p. 180.

[149] Source: Cal and Rose Samra, *More Holy Hilarity*, p. 128.

[150] Source: Rob Wood, editor, *It's All in the Game: Funny Happenings for Those Who Love Sports*, p. 44.

[151] Source: Sam Norkin, *Drawings, Stories*, p. 302.

[152] Source: Joe E. Brown, *Laughter is a Wonderful Thing*, p. 89.

[153] Source: Donald Richie, *Zen Inklings*, pp. 103-106.

[154] Source: Dave Rogers, *The Avengers*, p. 29.

[155] Source: Joe Hyams, *Zen in the Martial Arts*, pp. 73-74.

[156] Source: Steve Milton, *Skate Talk: Figure Skating in the Words of the Stars*, p. 209.

[157] Source: Sandra Bezic, *The Passion to Skate*, pp. 138-139.

[158] Source: David K. Wright, *Arthur Ashe: Breaking the Color Barrier in Tennis*, p. 54.

[159] Source: Sam Norkin, *Drawings, Stories*, p. 250.

[160] Source: Gene Ward and Dick Hyman, *Football Wit and Humor*, p. xii.

[161] Source: Donald J. Sobol, *Encyclopedia Brown's Book of Wacky Sports*, pp. 110-111.

[162] Source: Herma Silverstein, *Mary Lou Retton and the New Gymnasts*, p. 51.

[163] Source: Jayne Torvill and Christopher Dean, *Torvill and Dean*, p. 63.

[164] Source: Cal and Rose Samra, *More Holy Hilarity*, p. 128.

[165] Source: Albert Belle, *Don't Call Me Joey*, p. 16.

[166] Source: Leonard Feather and Jack Tracy, *Laughter from the Hip: The Lighter Side of Jazz*, pp. 70-71.

[167] Source: Kermit Schafer, *All Time Great Bloopers*, p. 16.

[168] Source: Joe Garagiola, *It's Anybody's Ballgame*, p. 52.

[169] Source: Richard Mackenzie, *A Wee Nip at the 19th Hole*, p. 112, plus the page before p. 1.

[170] Source: Barry Wilner, *Michelle Kwan: Star Figure Skater*, p. 56.

[171] Source: Beverley Smith, *Talking Figure Skating*, pp. 305-306.

[172] Source: Christine Brennan, *Inside Edge*, p. 217.

[173] Source: Barry Wilner, *Michelle Kwan: Star Figure Skater*, pp. 18, 42.

[174] Source: April Koral, *Florence Griffith Joyner: Track and Field Star*, p. 47.

[175] Source: Margaret Poynter, *Top 10 American Women's Figure Skaters*, pp. 23-24.

[176] Source: Jeff Savage, *Tiger Woods: King of the Course*, pp. 25-26.

[177] Source: Ray Buck, *Tiffany Chin: A Dream on Ice*, pp. 7-8, 45.

[178] Source: Ross R. Olney, *Lyn St. James: Driven to Be First*, pp. 35-36.

[179] Source: Dominique Moceanu, *Dominique Moceanu, An American Champion*, p. 70.

[180] Source: William R. Sanford and Carl R. Green, *Dorothy Hamill*, p. 15.

[181] Source: Ray Buck, *Tiffany Chin: A Dream on Ice*, p. 44.

[182] Source: Rachel Rutledge, *The Best of the Best in Gymnastics*, p. 29.

[183] Source: Hal Straus, editor, *Gymnastics Guide*, p. 307.

[184] Source: George Sullivan, *Any Number Can Play*, p. 77.

[185] Source: Jeff Savage, *Tiger Woods: King of the Course*, p. 17.

[186] Source: Christina Lessa, *Gymnastics Balancing Acts*, pp. 50-51.

[187] Source: William R. Sanford and Carl R. Green, *Dorothy Hamill*, pp. 22, 46.

[188] Source: Nancy H. Kleinbaum, *The Magnificent Seven*, p. 73.

[189] Source: Bill Barich, *The Sporting Life: Horses, Boxers, Rivers, and a Soviet Ballclub*, pp. 98-99.

[190] Source: Bart Conner, *Winning the Gold*, pp. 94-95.

[191] Source: Michael V. Uschan, *Male Olympic Champions*, p. 12.

[192] Source: Tara Lipinski, *Totally Tara: An Olympic Journey*, p. 140.

[193] Source: Bela Karolyi and Nancy Ann Richardson, *Feel No Fear*, pp. 157-158.

[194] Source: Tom Streissguth, *Jesse Owens*, pp. 54-55.

[195] Source: Peggy Fleming, *The Long Program*, p. 64.

[196] Source: Dwight Chapin, "The Olympic Game," *Playgirl*, January 1977.

[197] Source: Barbara Long, *Jim Thorpe: Legendary Athlete*, p. 13.

[198] Source: Cordell Brown, *I am What I am by the Grace of God*, pp. 26, 81.

[199] Source: Pete Donovan, *Carol Johnston: The One-Armed Gymnast*, pp. 7-8, 10, 12, 14-15, 34.

[200] Source: George Sullivan, *Any Number Can Play*, pp. 13-14.

[201] Source: Morris K. Udall, *Too Funny to be President*, pp. 100-101.

[202] Source: Betty Millsaps Jones, *Wonder Women of Sports*, pp. 47-51.

[203] Source: Jimmy Crum and Carole Gerber, *How About That!*, pp. 162-163.

[204] Source: Lee Kilduff, *Sports Heroines*, pp. 33, 35.

[205] Source: George Jessel, *This Way, Miss*, p. 184.

[206] Source: John A. Torres, *Greg Maddux: Ace!*, pp. 27, 51.

[207] Source: Michael J. Pellowski, *Baseball's Funniest People*, p. 31.

[208] Source: Fred Russell, teller, *Funny Thing About Sports*, pp. 50-51.

[209] Source: Art Linkletter, *I Wish I'd Said That!*, p. 48.

[210] Source: Joe Garagiola, *Baseball is a Funny Game*, p. 59.

[211] Source: Art Linkletter, *I Wish I'd Said That!*, pp. 48-49.

[212] Source: Elizabeth Schleichert, *Dave Bing: Basketball Great with a Heart*, pp. 29-30.

[213] Source: Peggy Fleming, *The Long Program*, p. 87.

[214] Source: Christina Lessa, *Women Who Win*, p. 26.

[215] Source: Barbara Long, *Jim Thorpe: Legendary Athlete*, pp. 37-38.

[216] Source: The NBC presentation of the 2000 Pontiac Women's Gymnastics Team Championships.

[217] Source: R.R. Knudson, *Babe Didrikson: Athlete of the Century*, p. 45.

[218] Source: Kerri Strug, *Landing on My Feet*, p. 168.

[219] Source: S.H. Burchard, *Tracy Austin*, pp. 53-56.

[220] Source: Karen Mueller Coombs, *Jackie Robinson: Baseball's Civil Rights Legend*, pp. 5ff.

[221] Source: Ross R. Olney, *Lyn St. James: Driven to Be First*, pp. 9-11.

[222] Source: Don Wade, *"And Then Arnie Told Chi Chi...,"* p. 199.

[223] Source: Bruce Adelson, *Grand Slam Trivia*, p. 36.

[224] Source: Ira L. Smith and H. Allen Smith, *Low and Inside*, pp. 42-43.

[225] Source: David Pietrusza, *The Boston Celtics Basketball Team*, p. 24.

[226] Source: Tara Lipinski and Emily Costello, *Tara Lipinski: Triumph on Ice*, pp. 10-11.

[227] Source: Donald J. Sobol, *Encyclopedia Brown's Book of the Wacky Outdoors*, pp. 82-85.

[228] Source: William R. Sanford and Carl R. Green, *Bill Pickett: African-American Rodeo Star*, pp. 5-6, 8.

[229] Source: Lynn Haney, *Ride 'em, Cowgirl!*, pp. 112-113.

[230] Source: Donald J. Sobol, *Encyclopedia Brown's Book of Wacky Sports*, pp. 13-14.

[231] Source: Bill Gutman, *The Harlem Globetrotters*, p. 41.

[232] Source: Gene Ward and Dick Hyman, *Football Wit and Humor*, pp. xiii-xiv.

[233] Source: Art Berke, *Babe Ruth*, p. 62.

[234] Source: Arna Bontemps, *Famous Negro Athletes*, p. 115.

[235] Source: Bob Uecker and Mickey Herskowitz, *Catcher in the Wry*, pp. 161-162.

[236] Source: Tom Gorman and Jerome Holtzman, *Three and Two!*, pp. 103-104.

[237] Source: Jocko Conlan and Robert W. Creamer, *Jocko*, pp. 94-96.

[238] Source: John C. Skipper, *Umpires*, p. 87.

[239] Source: Ira L. Smith and H. Allen Smith, *Low and Inside*, pp. 181-182.

[240] Source: Harry "Steamboat" Johnson, *Standing the Gaff*, p. 88.

[241] Source: Fred Russell, teller, *Funny Thing About Sports*, p. 53.

[242] Source: Jocko Conlan and Robert W. Creamer, *Jocko*, p. 98.

[243] Source: Joe Garagiola, *It's Anybody's Ballgame*, p. 62.

[244] Source: Ira L. Smith and H. Allen Smith, *Three Men on Third*, pp. 67-68.

[245] Source: Eric Gregg and Marty Appel, *Working the Plate*, p. 164.

[246] Source: Michael J. Pellowski, *Baseball's Funniest People*, pp. 20-21.

[247] Source: Elfi Schlegel and Claire Ross Dunn, *The Gymnastics Book*, p. 10.

[248] Source: Miriam Weiss Meyer, project editor, *Top Picks: People*, p. 14.

[249] Source: Margot Fortunato Galt, *Up to the Plate: The All American Girls Professional Baseball League*, pp. 10-11, 21, 93.

[250] Source: Michael Suponev, *Olga Korbut*, pp. 51-52.